AF800690

INVOLVED IN A TRUCKING WRECK IN OKLAHOMA?

Navigate Your Personal Injury Claim The Right Way

ATTORNEY JOE CARSON

Copyright © 2022 by Attorney Joe Carson

All rights reserved. No part of this publication may be reproduced, distributed, or transmitted in any form or by any means, including photocopying, recording, or other electronic or mechanical methods, without the prior written permission of the publisher, except in the case of brief quotations embodied in critical reviews and certain other noncommercial uses permitted by copyright law. For permission requests, write to the publisher, addressed "Attention: Permissions Coordinator," at the address below.

Jacobs & Whitehall
21750 Hardy Oak Blvd
Suite 104
#51700
San Antonio, Texas 78258
www.jacobsandwhitehall.com

Ordering Information:

Quantity sales. Special discounts are available on quantity purchases by corporations, associations, and others. For details, contact the publisher at the address above.

Orders by U.S. trade bookstores and wholesalers. Please contact Jacobs & Whitehall: Tel: (888) 991-2766 or visit www.jacobsandwhitehall.com.

Printed in the United States of America

Published in 2022

ISBN: 978-1-954506-37-4

ABOUT THE AUTHOR

Joe Carson was born and raised in Yukon, OK. He graduated from Oklahoma State University with a BS in Environmental Science and a Minor in Agriculture Economics. He received his Juris Doctor from Oklahoma City University in 2002. He is a member of the Oklahoma Bar Association, Oklahoma Association for Justice, and the Oklahoma County Bar Association, as well as the William J. Holloway, Jr. American Inn of Court and the American Association of Justice. He has been named to the Super Lawyer by his peers and has spoken on many topics in his industry, including (1) truck accident litigation, (2)

how to pick a jury, (3) Building Your Civil Trial Skills, Oklahoma Civil Discovery, (4) Challenges for Cause and Making Them Stick, and (5) Plaintiff's Personal Injury from Start to Finish. Joe was recently selected to OCU Law School Executive Board.

Joe has been practicing law in Oklahoma and across the United States for 18 years. His practice is primarily limited to personal injury and wrongful death cases arising from semi wrecks, car wrecks, motorcycle wrecks, airplane wrecks, defective products, and medical errors. Joe also handles insurance bad faith cases, as well as environmental and oil and gas litigation.

DEDICATION

This book is dedicated to all of my past clients who have taught me how to work hard and care for people in a way that I never dreamed possible. Thank you for trusting me with your case in the awful times after your tragic event. Without my past clients, I would not have the knowledge, ability, and skill to do what I do.

PREFACE

In a split second, one person's actions can change the path of another life forever. I wrote this book to help someone in need and to better explain what to expect when involved in a wreck with a semi. Hopefully, this book will make the process of making and litigating a claim a little easier and more understandable. This book would not have been possible without the help of a wonderful team to create, edit, and produce this book. I hope my experience and knowledge can help you during an extremely difficult time.

DISCLAIMER

This publication is intended to be used for educational purposes only. No legal advice is being given, and no attorney-client relationship is intended to be created by reading this material. The author assumes no liability for any errors or omissions or for how this book or its contents are used or interpreted, or for any consequences resulting directly or indirectly from the use of this book. For legal or any other advice, please consult an experienced attorney or the appropriate expert, who is aware of the specific facts of your case and is knowledgeable in the law in your jurisdiction.

WARHAWK LEGAL
127 NW 10th Street
Oklahoma City, OK 73103
(405) 397-1717
www.warhawklegal.com
joe@warhawklegal.com

Testimonials

"Joe Carson and the staff at Warhawk Legal are the best! They handled my case very professionally and kept me informed throughout the process. They were quick to respond to any questions, and I was always treated with kindness and respect. I highly recommend them!"

– Julie F.

****

"I am very appreciative to Joe Carson and his staff. He made a tough situation much easier. I am grateful to have come up on top in a situation where I felt like I was getting run over. Can't express how thankful my family is."

– Debbie H.

****

"Joe Carson and his staff are unbelievable. I had no idea what to do or where to turn and they calmed me down and helped me the entire time. Can't say enough good things about Joe."

– Pam G.

****

"Joe Carson and his staff were extremely helpful to me and my family during a difficult time. This could have been a confusing time for us, but with his help, it went very smoothly."

– Lateesha C.

****

"I was a nervous wreck and they settled my nerves and made me feel taken care of! I had no clue what was best or what to do and I feel like I was in the best hands I could've been in. Thank you, Mr. Carson and team!"

– Meredith Apple

****

"Joe is a great attorney! He helped me understand my options and get me the justice I was seeking."

– Jose C.

****

Table Of Contents

CHAPTER 1

WHAT IS PERSONAL INJURY LAW IN OKLAHOMA?

Personal injury law in Oklahoma is the area of law that covers accidents and injuries, caused by others, which cause you physical or emotional harm. This includes accidents caused by large commercial vehicles or large trucks, including semi-trucks.

The following list includes a few of the situations in which we have successfully pursued compensation for individuals with personal injury claims: Vehicle Wrecks, Trucking Wrecks, Motorcycle Wrecks, Medical Negligence, Nursing Home Negligence, Wrongful Death, Pedestrian Accidents, Bicycle Accidents, Dog Bites, Premises Liability, Product Liability, Construction Accidents, Workers' Compensation, and Aviation Law.

While the State of Oklahoma is a wonderful place to live and enjoy life, unfortunately, bad things can and do happen on the roadways. According to the Oklahoma Highway Safety Office (OHSO) which compiles crash data from all law enforcement agencies in Oklahoma, there were 12,304 people injured in motor-vehicle crashes in 2019, and it is worth noting that this figure may not be all inclusive since there is a likelihood that some crashes with minor injuries aren't reported to law enforcement. Sadly, 640 lives were taken in Oklahoma motor vehicle accidents in 2019. Of those injured in Oklahoma crashes in 2019, 3,685 people were injured in Oklahoma County, Cleveland County, and Canadian County. Those statistics, including those from the Oklahoma City Metro, include crashes related to speed, alcohol, drugs, distracted drivers, and drowsy drivers to name a few; 291 injuries were speed related, 183 injuries were alcohol related, 39 injuries were drug-related, 408 injuries were related to distracted driving, and 45 injuries were related to drowsy drivers. Holiday travel is a time when traveling frequency increases, which increases the frequency of crashes. On New Year's Day of 2018, there were 129 crashes involving injuries or fatalities. Furthermore, during the 2018 Christmas season, there were 166 crashes involving injuries or fatalities. These harrowing statistics suggest Oklahomans should maintain attentiveness, sobriety, and always be on the defense while behind the wheel.

When you or a family member is injured in a trucking accident in Oklahoma, there are multiple categories of monetary damages for which you may be compensated relating to the lasting and sometimes permanent effects of the injury. When one is injured, he or she may need to consult a medical professional and may have to undergo surgery and/or treatment. You have to pay for doctor's visits, prescriptions, surgeries, and treatments. The injured person may be prescribed medicines, may have to take off work, may be unable to perform the same work they did before the injury, or may have to pay for a funeral under less fortunate circumstances. All of those products and services will cost money, and the cost of healthcare continues to grow. It will be challenging to make doctor visits have surgeries performed, or recover while continuing to work, so you may be forced to take time off and could lose wages you would have otherwise earned had you not been injured. Monetary damages are also known as economic damages and are intended to compensate the injured party for expenses incurred as a result of the injury. An injury from a commercial vehicle or large truck may cause life-changing injuries that you carry for an extended period of time.

You may also be entitled to non-economic damages such as physical pain and suffering and/or mental pain and suffering after a semi-truck accident. Physical pain and suffering refer to the actual physical pain resulting from the plaintiff's injuries. Emotional pain and suffering refer to the mental toll the injuries have taken on the plaintiff. For example, mental anguish, emotional distress, loss of enjoyment of life, anxiety, fear, humiliation, shock, and depression are all types of emotional pain and suffering for which you may be compensated.

The usual basis for liability in a trucking accident claim is negligence. Negligence assigns liability based upon whether someone owes a duty of care to another person and whether that person breaches that duty by not meeting the required standard of conduct. The fact that you were injured, perhaps by another's unreasonable conduct, does not mean you are automatically entitled to compensation. You must prove the other person was negligent. Negligence is the failure of someone to exercise ordinary care to avoid injury to another person or property. In order to prove the truck driver's negligence was the cause of your injuries, you must prove the following elements: (1) the truck driver owed a duty of care to you, (2) the truck driver breached that duty, and (3) the truck driver's breach directly and proximately caused your injury.

In a typical trucking accident injury case, you are seeking compensation from the trucking company's insurance company. For example, if a driver of a vehicle is injured and goes to the emergency room because the driver of the truck swerved into the oncoming lane while texting, it could be argued that the texting driver owed a duty of care to the plaintiff and caused damages when he or she breached that duty by texting while driving. All insurance companies employ attorneys whose sole purpose is to defend against these types of claims. This is why it is important to consult with an experienced trucking accident attorney as soon as possible following an accident.

Additionally, activities that could be considered extremely dangerous, such as transporting ultrahazardous chemicals or handling explosives, might impose strict liability.

You may be asking yourself, when should you reach out to an attorney about a potential trucking accident injury claim? The general rule is the sooner the better, and, as long as the statute of limitations for your claim has not lapsed, you can bring a claim.

Depending on the type of claim you have, the statute of limitations sets a maximum time limit for when a claim can be brought. In most trucking accident cases in Oklahoma, the statute of limitations is set at two years from the date of the accident or injury giving rise to the claim. However, there are certain instances in Oklahoma where the statute of limitations or the requirement to give notice of a claim can be as little as one year or possibly shorter.

CHAPTER 2

STEPS TO TAKE TO GIVE TRUCKING ACCIDENT CASE THE BEST POSSIBLE OUTCOME

What To Do After a Truck Accident

When speaking to the police at the scene of a trucking accident, you should be honest, tell them your version of the events, let them know whether you are hurt, and tell them whether you were wearing a seatbelt. If you can think of any other cause of the wreck other than the truck driver, then make sure to identify that with the police. If possible, you should take photographs of the scene of the accident, including the semi-truck that hit you, your vehicle, any debris on the street, any skid marks on the street, and the surrounding area (e.g., the intersection where the wreck occurred).

If you speak with the truck driver at the scene, be polite, but don't admit fault. Be advised that anything you say to the other party, or the police officer could be used against you at a later time in your civil case. You should collect the other party's insurance information, as well as take a picture of their insurance card and driver's license. You should also collect the name, address, and phone number of anyone who claims to have witnessed the wreck or might have any important information or evidence. Believe it or not, police officers often omit witness contact information from their reports, so it is imperative that someone obtains it at the time of the wreck.

If your medical condition is such that you feel an ambulance ride to the hospital is necessary, then certainly take an ambulance. If you can go to the hospital on your own, then do so. Broken bones, significant pain, lightheadedness, heart palpations, tightness in your chest, and any other symptoms that concern you definitely warrant a trip to the emergency room. However, it is often the case that injury symptoms may not manifest themselves until a few hours or days after the wreck when the adrenaline from the traumatic experience has dissipated. If you do not notice any injuries while at the scene of the wreck, tell the officer that you are unsure whether you have sustained an injury, as this will hopefully prompt the officer to note there is possible injury (rather than no injury).

Once you are being medically evaluated, make sure to be honest with the medical practitioners, identify the areas of pain or injury, notify the doctor of any preexisting conditions, and ensure that your injuries are being documented. If you don't document your injuries, then the insurance adjusters and the lawyers working for them will say the injuries don't exist. After you've been released from the hospital, follow up with your primary care physician. In Oklahoma, some primary care physicians will not see a motor vehicle accident client because they're not set up to handle the billing aspect of the case. Under these circumstances, you should seek out specific facilities and medical practitioners that treat victims of automobile wrecks. An attorney in the area should be able to provide you with a list of providers who will treat you.

It is also critical not to let a gap in treatment arise because you think you'll get better. Trucking company insurance companies and defense attorneys will use a gap in treatment against you. The best advice is to follow the doctor's orders, go to all of your follow-up appointments, and identify every injury, even if it's not bothering you as severely as your other injuries. If the doctor recommends additional treatment or diagnostic testing (e.g. physical therapy, MRI, CT scan, injection), then follow those recommendations without delay.

In conclusion, seek medical treatment immediately if you've been injured in a trucking accident. Your health and well-being are of the utmost importance. Sometimes people don't notice symptoms of an injury immediately after the accident and start to feel it hours or days after. Some don't seek medical treatment immediately because they don't want to incur the expense of medical bills. However, if your injury is not adequately documented in medical records it will be very difficult for you to prove your claim even if you were injured.

Continue treatment and recommendations your provider(s) gives you. A significant gap in treatment can negatively affect your case.

What Is The Statute Of Limitations For A Trucking Accident Case In Oklahoma?

The statute of limitations generally refers to the time limit on filing a lawsuit. The statute of limitations for a trucking accident case in Oklahoma is usually two years from the date of the injury. If the statute of limitations (or notice requirement) is missed, then you will be forever barred from making a claim. If you are unsure as to whether or not your case needs to be filed within a certain amount of time, I encourage you to contact an attorney immediately. You do not want to call a lawyer at the last minute; in fact, most lawyers will not take a case if they have fewer than two weeks to prepare and file it.

CHAPTER 3

FACTORS OF A VIABLE TRUCKING ACCIDENT CASE

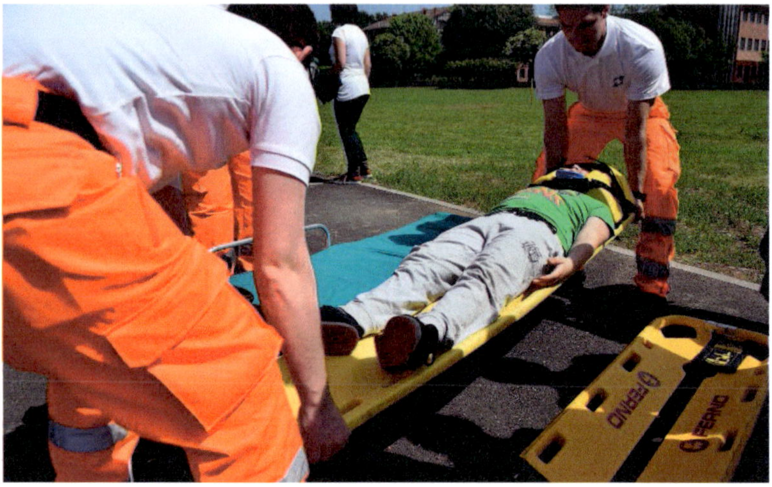

Just because you have been injured in a trucking accident, does not mean you will have a personal injury case. I was trained that in order to make a viable personal injury case you must have three legs of a stool: (1) liability, (2) damages, and (3) the ability to collect.

Liability: The truck driver was negligent and caused your injuries.

Damages: Medical expenses, lost income, pain, and suffering. There has to be damages. Just because someone did something wrong does not mean they have to pay you money. The wrongful act must cause damages.

Ability to Collect: You may have a case where liability is clear, damages are significant but there is no insurance or any other way to collect money for your client. In other words, you can't get blood out of a turnip.

You must have all three legs of the stool for a trucking accident injury case to be viable.

Truckers are required by law to adhere to certain rules and regulations which don't apply to the general public. If a tractor-trailer is involved in your wreck, it is extremely important to involve an attorney quickly so a proper investigation can be completed, and evidence can be preserved. This will sometimes include using a wreck investigator who can go to the scene and document the evidence as well as attempt to download critical evidence and information from the tractor before it is destroyed.

Will My Preexisting Condition Preclude Me From Bringing A Viable Trucking Injury Case?

Do not give up on your trucking accident case just because you have a preexisting medical condition. Under Oklahoma law, you are allowed to recover for any aggravation of a preexisting medical condition. In fact, preexisting medical conditions sometimes better enable an attorney to explain to the jury the specific ways in which the client has been injured by the incident. For example, someone with a preexisting injury may be more susceptible to an injury from a particular wreck. Someone that has injured their neck prior to a wreck might be more prone to injury than someone with no prior injury.

What Compensation/Damages Can I Seek In My Trucking Accident Injury Case?

When negotiating a settlement with the trucking company's insurance representatives, our goal is to have our clients compensated for *all* damages associated with their claim. This can include medical expenses, pain and suffering, loss of wages, punitive damages (if applicable), loss of consortium, future losses, and future medical expenses. This will also vary case by case as some damages and injuries are worse than others, especially in trucking accident cases.

How Is The Worth Of A Trucking Injury Case Determined?

I get asked all the time "what is my case worth" or "how much will you be able to get me." These questions rely heavily on the extent of your damages. Any lawyer who promises you a certain amount of money for your trucking accident case, when you first meet, is just blowing smoke and should be a red flag. I would suspect they are simply trying to convince you to hire them, and I would also suggest you run as fast as you can. Simply put, there is no way to establish what your trucking accident case is worth until you have completed your medical treatment, identified all of your injuries, and done an investigation; all of which takes time. My standard response to questions relating to financial compensation and recovery is that I will work as hard as I can to get you all the money you are legally entitled to recover from the at-fault party. Once

I have more knowledge as to your damages, liability, and other facts, I will be in a better position to estimate the value of your claim. I will usually provide a range of possible outcomes, understanding there is no way to accurately predict the exact value of your case. The only way to determine for sure what your case is worth is to ask 12 jurors to make that determination. Even then, two very similar cases can have drastically different values depending on the parties involved, the facts of the case, and the injuries sustained.

How Are The Costs of Long-Term Care, Future Surgeries, And Treatments Calculated In Serious Injury Cases?

We hire experts who are highly qualified to calculate future costs. Our experts analyze information from interviews, medical records, educational material, publications, studies, consultations with other professionals, medical providers, and diagnostic evaluations to assess clients' abilities and needs. These experts are very good at using the information they gather and putting together a future life care plan or estimating future lost wages.

CHAPTER 4

HOW DOES COMPARATIVE NEGLIGENCE AFFECT A TRUCKING INJURY CASE?

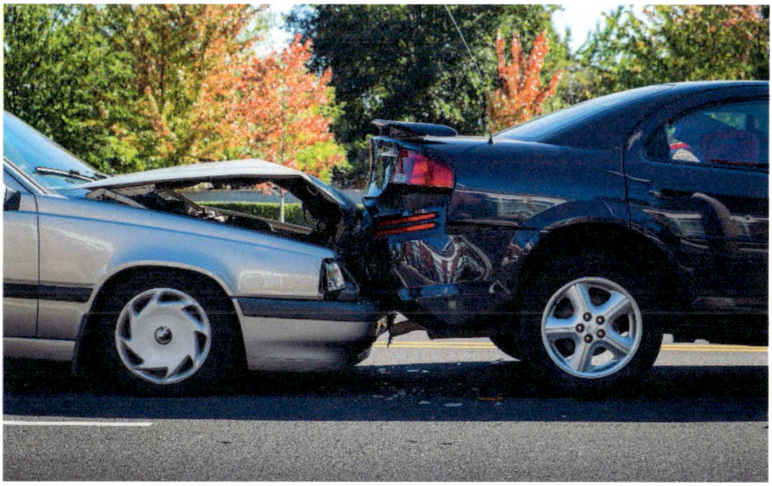

Comparative negligence is when the plaintiff is partially responsible for the incident that caused his or her injuries. In a trucking accident case, this could reduce the compensation to which they are entitled if their negligent actions increased the probability of the accident. Insurance companies and defense attorneys will almost always attempt to establish comparative negligence and place a percentage of fault on the plaintiff.

Oklahoma is a comparative fault state, which means that the responsibility of each person in a trucking accident is assessed to determine fault based on each person's role in the accident. Each person's actions leading up to an accident will affect the amount of compensation they receive for their injuries.

Comparative negligence will not bar recovery unless the injured plaintiff's negligence is greater than the negligence of the defendant. 23 O.S. § 13. If a defendant argues the plaintiff was comparatively negligent then the defendant has the burden to prove that plaintiff contributed to the incident. Where contributory negligence is shown on the injured person's part, the amount of recovery will be reduced in proportion to the contributory negligence. 23 O.S. § 14. Oklahoma's Comparative Negligence rule allows the plaintiff to recover as long as he or she isn't determined to be more than 50% at fault. For example, the driver of a vehicle was injured in a vehicle collision where another vehicle's driver was determined to be 51% at fault and the injured plaintiff was determined to be 49% at fault. In a suit by the injured plaintiff against the other vehicle's driver, the plaintiff is permitted to recover 51% of the amount of damages because his or her total damages are reduced by 49%, which is his or her allocated share of negligence. A plaintiff generally benefits greatly from counsel by a personal injury attorney experienced in establishing the fault of a negligent party who caused the injuries. And, importantly, an experienced trucking accident injury attorney will argue against any defense where the other side attempts to say that you, the injured plaintiff, caused or contributed to the incident.

Punitive Damages In Oklahoma

Some trucking accident injury cases call for an award of punitive damages. Punitive damages are different from economic damages and non-economic damages in a couple of ways. First, punitive damages aren't awarded to compensate the injured. They are awarded to punish the defendant's conduct and to discourage others from performing similar acts. Punitive damages are sometimes appropriate in personal injury cases where the jury is persuaded that the defendant has acted in reckless disregard for the rights of others or where the defendant has acted with malice. If the jury decides that the defendant did not act with malice or reckless disregard for the rights of others, then punitive damages will not be awarded. Reckless disregard describes conduct where the defendant was either aware, or did not care, that there was a substantial and unnecessary risk that his or her conduct would cause serious injury to others. Malice describes either hatred, spite, ill-will, or other intentional wrongful act without justification.

When the jury decides the defendant has acted with malice or reckless disregard for the rights of others, the next step is for the jury to determine the amount of the award. According to 23 O.S. § 9.1, in determining the amount, the jury can consider the following factors: (1) The seriousness of the hazard to the public arising from the defendant's misconduct; (2) The profitability of the misconduct to the defendant; (3) How long the conduct lasted and whether it is likely to continue; (4) Whether there were attempts to conceal the misconduct; (5) How aware the defendant was of the conduct and its consequences and how aware the defendant was of the hazard and of its excessiveness;

(6) The attitude and conduct of the defendant upon finding out about the misconduct/hazard; (7) The financial condition of the defendant; (8) The number and level of employees involved in causing or concealing the misconduct (if the defendant is a corporation or entity). Further, depending on whether the defendant's conduct is determined to be malicious or with reckless disregard for the rights of others, punitive damages can be capped at certain levels in Oklahoma. An experienced personal injury attorney will know how to analyze your situation and tell you whether punitive damages should be pursued.

Additional Considerations

A few years ago, the Oklahoma legislature passed a law that allows doctors, hospitals, physical therapists, and other medical practitioners to file liens on cases. A lien looks like a nasty document that affects your house and makes most people mad when they receive them in the mail, but, ultimately, what it does is put everyone in the case—including the insurance company, defendant, you, and your lawyer—on notice that there is a third-party medical practitioner making a claim against the settlement proceeds. The lien does not affect your house, property, vehicle, or bank account.

The purpose behind this law is to enable medical practitioners to render medical services to potentially uninsured people with the expectation that they will get paid from the case. At some point, when the case resolves, attorneys will attempt to negotiate the lien. If you receive a lien in the mail, there is no need to stress about it because it's what medical practitioners do in order to protect their interests for the services they render. If not for the lien statute, it would be difficult to find a medical practitioner willing to treat you as a result of an injury sustained in an accident.

CHAPTER 5

REASONS FOR OKLAHOMA TRUCKING ACCIDENTS

With several major thoroughfares crisscrossing Oklahoma, it makes for numerous trucks passing through the state.

In Oklahoma, we have interstate highways I-35 and I-40 running north to south and east to west. According to the federal government, we also have one of the most dangerous highways in the country. Highway 9, running through Cleveland County, is ranked in the top five most dangerous highways in the country.

When the federal government allows speed limits to increase, Oklahoma is usually one of the first in line to increase. Right now, we have 80 miles an hour limits in some locations and many interstates are 75.

With a significant number of tractor-trailer trucks crossing the state, along with the extreme weather conditions and high speeds, it makes for a lot of truck litigation.

Significant causes of tractor-trailer wrecks in Oklahoma include:

1. Driver error
2. Driving or driver training
3. Equipment failure
4. Company issues - failure to train, supervise, oversee
5. Substance abuse - alcohol and drugs

The number one reason is driver error, including everything from driver fatigue to distraction. Falling asleep, drowsy driving, cellphones, computers, GPS devices, and radios are all very hazardous when driving a tractor-trailer. Driver error also includes the driver's ability to make decisions, such as traveling too fast for road or weather conditions, misjudging the speed of a vehicle, following too close, etc.

The number two reason for accidents, driver training, is an elementary principle. Are these drivers adequately trained? Are they properly supervised and getting the safety training they need? Should the company be more interested in making sure their drivers are safe? All drivers, even ones that have been driving for many years, should continually be trained and refreshed on safety.

Number three, equipment failures, are one of the leading causes, including:

- Tie-down failures
- Poorly maintained or faulty brakes
- Worn or improperly inflated tires
- Malfunctioning or misaligned under-ride rails
- Unbalanced cargo

I once had a case where the wreck occurred because a tie-down broke off a flatbed trailer being pulled through Oklahoma. The driver failed to properly inspect the tie-downs pursuant to Federal Motor Carrier Safety Standards. When the tie-down broke, part of the load fell off the bed and my client hit it, causing him to go airborne into a ditch. He had back surgery because of his injuries. This was a punitive damage case. We demonstrated the driver should have inspected the strap within about five miles of where the wreck occurred. Had he followed the proper rules and regulations, the wreck could have been prevented.

Number four is company priorities. Often, these companies are more interested in making money rather than following proper safety policies and procedures, which leads to more wrecks. The goal of these companies is to get loads where they need to be as fast as they can. This policy oftentimes causes their drivers to neglect or ignore safety requirements such as a driver's rest or break times required by federal law. If they would follow safety rules, regulations, and procedures, they would find their company would be more productive and safer. In the long run, probably be more profitable as well. Safety should be the number one priority instead of getting goods and people where they need to be as fast as possible or getting drivers as many hours and miles as they can.

Number five, substance abuse, is undoubtedly self-explanatory. If you're drunk or on drugs, don't drive. It affects your ability to perceive and react. When you're driving a massive tractor-trailer down the highway, anything that affects your ability to perceive a dangerous condition and react should be eliminated at all costs. That's just common sense.

CHAPTER 6

TRUCKING ACCIDENT INJURIES

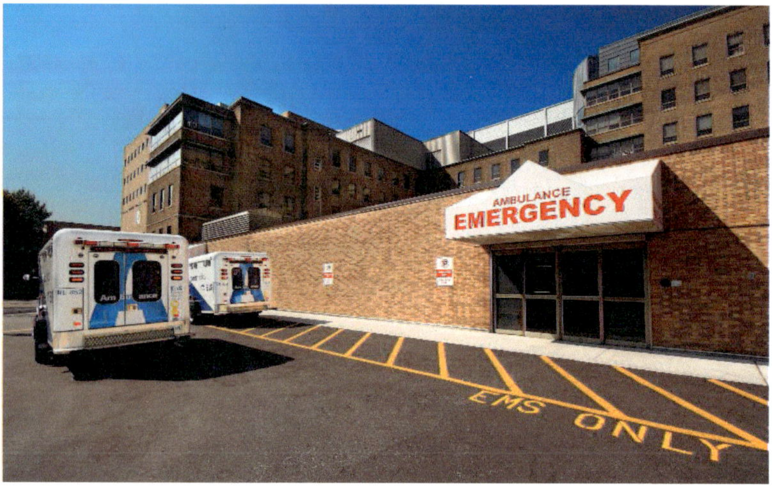

The most significant difference I see between a trucking wreck and a regular car wreck is the injuries associated with the accident. You might ask yourself, "Why is that? Why do you see more significant injuries associated with tractor-trailer wrecks than regular run-of-the-mill car wrecks?" The difference is the size and weight of the tractor and trailer. For example, a standard car wreck may involve two 6,000-pound vehicles, whereas a tractor with a loaded trailer may weigh 60,000 pounds. You can see the difference. The injury-causing mechanism is that bigger, heavier trucks cause more damage than regular automobile vehicles.

We also see many injuries associated with underride or override collisions. Underride is when a vehicle hits the trailer and goes under it, causing decapitation-type injuries. An override injury is when the front bumper of the semi does not line up with the back bumper of a passenger vehicle, so it overrides and causes cab intrusion.

Many countries have implemented federal regulations forcing the manufacturers of tractors to lower or adjust their front bumpers to align with passenger vehicles properly. This measure decreases the type of injury and the severity of injuries in override accidents. We have not done that here in the United States for some reason.

We see serious injuries, from soft tissue injuries to death. The more common injuries we see are:

- Internal injuries
- Catastrophic brain injuries

- Internal bleeding
- Broken bones
- Head injuries
- Spine Injuries

Now and then, we even have burn cases that occur as a result of a fire.

CHAPTER 7

GATHERING EVIDENCE

Getting a lawyer involved early on with tractor-trailer wreck cases is essential. We often need to go to the scene to investigate; potentially even hire an accident investigator, reconstructionist, or biomechanical engineer to gather evidence. These professionals document the site by looking for evidence such as skid, scuff, gouge marks, or anything on the physical highway to identify specific points in the chain of events of the wreck. We can actually place where the truck was at any given time by recreating what occurred.

It is essential to get to the scene of the accident to document everything that can be used later. This includes taking photos of the accident and the vehicles involved, identifying independent witnesses, and downloading the black boxes from the vehicles. You may be surprised how much information is available based on the download of electronic modules or various recording devices in some vehicles.

Investigating a semi wreck as early as possible is very important. Many times we have received a call concerning a wreck that occurred 18 months earlier and much of the evidence has been destroyed or lost. The vehicles aren't available. No one ever did a download of the vehicles. We can't find them or photograph them. Perhaps not destroyed in an evil manner, but the evidence disappears or is no longer available to you as time goes on. You need everything collected, even if you don't think you will use it. It's better to get it now in case you need it later.

You can spend thousands, even tens of thousands of dollars, on accident reconstructionists.

So, the first question you need to answer is, does this case justify the experience associated with an accident reconstructionist? If it does, the key is getting them to the scene fast.

There are a lot of reconstructionists in the state of Oklahoma that do this type of work. It isn't difficult to get a hold of them and get them out to the scene. Most of them know what they're doing and don't need their hand held. You just give them the accident investigation report and cut them loose. Provide them with a scope of work and what you need.

First, they will probably go to the scene, photographing, and collecting evidence. They will go to the vehicles, measuring and photographing, potentially videotaping them. They may even use survey equipment to make darn sure you have the information preserved for use at a later time.

Once the reconstructionist finishes with the scene, they can let you know if they believe the case warrants making a claim. I almost always use accident reconstructionists, even if we don't have them do a

100% workup and reconstruction of an accident. If the case justifies it, we like to have them at the scene as soon as possible after a wreck to use them later if we need to. If you end up going to trial or needing to reconstruct the accident, they have everything they need to do it. They can prepare evidence or demonstrative exhibits to get the case ready for trial at a later date.

CHAPTER 8

LIABLE PARTIES

The truck driver and trucking company are the people we always look to name as potential defendants in a semi-truck wreck. We can potentially look to the owner of the tractor or trailer, the shipper, the broker, or other third parties that may have caused or contributed to the wreck, such as other motorists or someone in charge of maintenance of the vehicle. We might look to a manufacturer of the tractor, trailer, or part manufacturer for equipment failures.

As things develop and change over the years, this approach has evolved. When I first started practicing law, we consistently named the insurance carrier as a named party in trucking litigation cases. We still do this in some situations, but generally, we don't as often as we used to.

What we might do in one case, we might not do in another. You always want to look for all things that cause or contribute to a wreck. Then identify why the accident occurred and who caused or contributed to it. In one case, you could have a manufacturer at fault, and in another case, a maintenance company or just the driver. The facts of the case determine who you need to look for to correctly identify each entity that caused or contributed to the wreck.

In Oklahoma, we are a comparative negligence state. We must identify each and every entity or person who caused or contributed to the wreck. We need to distinguish the percentage they're at fault. If we leave someone out, that's a percentage in which our client might go uncompensated. Pursuant to the current law in Oklahoma, the defendants are usually only responsible for the portion of the negligence they caused in the wreck.

Years ago, we had joint and several liabilities. If someone caused even 1% of the wreck, they had to pay for the whole thing. This may sound unjust and inequitable, but it helped decrease litigation and helped the injured person significantly. Now we go through and identify every entity person. There's a long list of who they could be, and we have to get them all involved. This creates more litigation, as well as causes the cases to be more difficult, costly, and time-consuming than what they used to be.

You do not always have to sue the driver in Oklahoma, but I do. I want to have the driver represented by a lawyer I can contact. Someone to issue discovery to, as well as deposition notices and subpoenas, and not worry about tracking them down across the country. For this reason, I always name the driver for litigation purposes. Often, we find naming the driver avoids diversity jurisdiction, so we keep the case in state court, not federal court.

If the driver is an independent contractor, we have to do our due diligence and dig in to find out more about the driver's history. We try to match Department of Transportation (DOT) numbers with police reports and what's on the Safety and Fitness Electronic Records (SAFER) website to identify who these people are and how they may relate to others.

From doing this type of litigation on a regular basis, we see companies that go in and out of business and do different things to bypass costs, as well as rules and regulations. We start to see patterns of what I call gypsy companies. They start running and operating under a particular name until they get shut down, then they start another entity under a different DOT number, right out of the same post office box.

You always want to do your due diligence anytime you have an independent contractor involved in a wreck. You want to name them. You might even trigger another insurance policy or save yourself a big headache later when the shipper or company you sue points their finger at the other entity.

The company may say, "We had nothing to do with them." We see this more and more with companies like Amazon. There is an entity driving a truck labeled Amazon, but they have nothing to do with Amazon other than hauling their product? Can Amazon get rid of the liability for hauling their goods by retaining a third party to do that? It all boils down to the facts of the case and the law in the particular jurisdiction in which the wreck occurred.

Out-of-state trucking companies do not hurt your case. Most trucking cases that we handle involve out-of-state companies and out-of-state drivers. We even have handled cases with companies out of Canada and Mexico.

The only thing that occurs with an out-of-state defendant is it might affect the venue in which your case is handled. For example, you might not be in Cleveland or Canadian County, State of Oklahoma courts. You might end up in a federal courthouse.

In Oklahoma, the jurisdictional long-arm statute allows us to reach out and grab anyone that has the minimum contacts necessary to bring a case. Driving a tractor-trailer on the roads through the state of Oklahoma provides for the minimum contacts in order to bring them to court here.

CHAPTER 9

POTENTIAL CLAIMS

If you've been involved in an accident with a large truck, there are several claims we look to bring:

- Negligence
- Negligence per se
- Negligent hiring, training, and supervision
- Negligent maintenance
- Product liability
- Negligent entrustment

We will potentially include a claim for punitive damages if the facts warrant making those allegations.

You probably at least have a claim of negligence. A truck driver has a duty to operate the tractor-trailer in a non-negligent manner. They owe a duty to drive safely, and when they breach that duty and cause you harm, a negligence claim is warranted.

We certainly would look at a negligence per se claim. For example, if they were driving recklessly—speeding or running a red light—if they did something that violated a statute or ordinate, we could make the argument that the violation of that statute or ordinance was the cause of the wreck. In that situation, we don't have to prove negligence. All we have to prove is that they've violated that statute or ordinance and that violation harmed you. This makes the case that much easier to prove.

We might include a manufacturer or product liability claim if a product fails. Due to case law in Oklahoma, we may allege negligent hiring, training, and supervision. Depending on the case and the facts, defense -attorneys may try to admit the truck driver was in the course and scope of their employment, then ask the courts to dismiss those claims.

We may also include a negligent entrustment claim. The case law in Oklahoma indicates that if you have a negligent entrustment claim, you can get into other discovery issues such as whether the truck driver was even qualified or adequately trained, etc.

In Oklahoma, if you are the spouse or loved one of someone who has been killed in an accident, you may bring a lawsuit on behalf of the estate of the deceased person. The estate makes the argument for the lawsuit and brings the case for all damages associated with it. You may potentially be appointed the personal representative or the special administrator of the deceased's estate, bringing a claim for all damages associated with the trucking wreck.

Often, we bring a separate case contained within a wrongful death case. You would potentially be the representative of the estate, and then we may have an individual claim associated with your loss of love and compassion for the death of your loved one.

CHAPTER 10

INSURANCE AND DEFENSE ATTORNEYS' STRATEGIES TO AVOID PAYING CLIENTS

Insurance companies and defense attorneys will do anything they can to point the finger at you or a third party in order to minimize their exposure or liability. For example, they might blame you for faking or malingering, try to convince the jury that your injuries were pre-existing rather than caused by the incident in question, or even argue that an intervening event such as a fall or another auto wreck caused your injuries.

Another tactic used by defense attorneys and insurance companies is to delay cases with the goal of pushing you to the point where you simply give up and do whatever is necessary to end the case. Defense attorneys bill by the hour. That being said, they will find any reason to drag out litigation. Remember, the longer a case lasts the more money defense attorneys will make.

Another strategy employed by insurance companies and defense attorneys is to attack you personally and paint you in a negative light. They might also use the defense medical examination as a way to poke holes in your case or use your past medical history against you. Often, the defense can rely upon these hired doctors to provide a medical opinion that minimizes your injuries or need for future treatment. It is your lawyer's job to cross-examine these paid defense experts and build an arsenal against them. However, these defense doctors are trained expert witnesses and they often do a good job of minimizing or destroying a plaintiff's case.

Another technique used by insurance companies and defense attorneys is called an offer to confess judgment. There are a couple of different mechanisms by which they use this, which are set out in Oklahoma Statutes. Ultimately, the defense attorney may file an offer to confess judgment whereby they offer a certain amount of money, and you have a certain amount of time to accept their offer. An offer to confess judgment must be accepted within a certain time period. If the time period lapses without an acceptance, or if you deny or decline that offer and do not get a better verdict at trial, then you could potentially be on the hook for the other side's attorney fees and costs, or a portion thereof. In essence, the offer to confess is just another arrow in their quiver to shoot at you in order to pressure you into an unreasonable settlement.

CHAPTER 11

WHEN TO SETTLE A TRUCKING ACCIDENT INJURY CASE

There are multiple reasons why it is a good idea to settle a trucking accident injury case. If I have a client who, I am confident, will not make a good witness, one who does not want to file a lawsuit, or, a client who has a background that could negatively impact their case, then I might advise them against pursuing a lawsuit. However, if I have a good client with a good case with enough damages to justify a lawsuit, I may suggest proceeding with a lawsuit or trial. In each case, I review the estimated costs of a lawsuit and trial, as well as the risks associated with pursuing a lawsuit or going to trial with my client. As my client, I want you to know the good, the bad, and the ugly regarding litigation and trial. Defense attorneys and insurance carriers are trained to dig into your past and bring up things that are absolutely not relevant to the case—things that embarrass you and paint you in a bad light before a jury. I believe that one of the most important requirements of going to trial is to make sure that the client is a good and likeable person. If a jury does not like a plaintiff, then it is very hard to convince a jury to help a client.

In evaluating a trucking accident case for potential litigation, we also want to decide whether there is a 'mad' factor, which means any reason a jury might get angry. For example, it's unlikely that a jury would be mad at a 70-year- old church-going grandmother of 10 who simply made a mistake and bumped the rear end of a vehicle. It's a lot more likely that a jury would be upset at a truck driver who caused a wreck as a result of using methamphetamine. If a jury gets mad, they are more likely to render a significant verdict for the claimant. If a jury doesn't have a reason to be angry or thinks the defendant made a simple mistake, then the jury is more likely to minimize the damages they award you.

After evaluating a settlement offer and analyzing the probable outcome of the trucking accident case, we will decide whether to pursue litigation. If your case is worth $15,000, the insurance company has offered $10,000, and it will cost $10,000 to litigate your case, then I will likely tell you that it isn't economical to litigate your case. We must consider the merits and value of the case in order to justify the time, expense, and risk of trial. Although many trucking accident cases do not end up in a trial, it is important to note we prepare every case as if it will end up going to trial from the very beginning.

How Are Settlement Funds Disbursed?

Once we resolve your trucking accident case, it may take weeks (or in some situations months) in order to collect the money. Once the money is collected, it will be deposited into our trust account to allow the bank to collect the funds. During that time, we will negotiate medical expenses. In addition, attorney fees, costs, medical liens, certain health insurance payments, expenses you direct us to pay, and any other expense that's associated with your claim that by a contract you owe, will be paid from the settlement amount. The remaining balance will be paid to you.

You are required to pay medical liens and certain amounts some health insurance companies pay. There are some situations where you may choose to not pay certain medical expenses. Should you choose to not pay some of the medical bills with your settlement money, you would still be legally responsible for paying the remaining amount at some point should the providers attempt to collect on the bills. Some clients choose to pay for the medical expenses as they arise or as the medical provider attempts to collect a payment, because, at that point, they may be better able to negotiate the amount the medical provider will accept as a full and final payment.

CHAPTER 12

WHEN A TRUCKING ACCIDENT INJURY CASE GOES TO LITIGATION

Insurance adjusters are trained to look for ways to not pay you, and they will dispute liability even when liability is clear. They will try to blame you for the truck wreck and the injuries you sustained and do anything they can to move the focus away from any evidence of negligence or recklessness on behalf of their insured. Cases that do go to litigation usually involve disputes over liability or disputes regarding the reasonableness and/or necessity of medical treatment. With that said, we may take a case to trial simply because we believe the case is worth significantly more than what's being offered by the insurance company.

Although we cannot predict with 100 percent certainty what the jury will decide, we can come up with a probable outcome based on our education and experience in the field over the past 20 years. We keep track of every verdict in the state of Oklahoma in order to evaluate cases for litigation. Certainly, there are never any guarantees, and a jury can award more or less than what we expect. The choice to proceed to trial will always be that of the client. Our job is to provide all of the available information to you so you can make an educated choice about whether or not to go to trial.

What Can I Expect If My Case Goes To Litigation?

Once we decide to proceed with litigation, we will draft a lawsuit wherein we outline the facts and allegations of the case. If it is filed in federal court, it is called a complaint. If it's filed in state court, it is called a petition. Once the case has been assigned to a specific judge, we will issue summons and serve the lawsuit upon the defendants. In most cases, a defendant is given 20 days to respond with an answer to the complaint or petition. In the answer, the defendant will either admit or deny our allegation in the petition. This will frame the issues that will be litigated. If the defendant admits to the allegations, then litigation won't be necessary to prove those allegations. If the defendant denies the allegations, then the issues will need to be litigated.

At this point, the discovery phase of litigation begins. We will send written discovery (i.e., interrogatories, requests for production of documents, and requests for admissions) to the other side, and vice versa. We will properly respond to the questions and produce the discoverable documents requested by the other side. The discovery phase is broad, and, in general, the other side can request many things that may or may not be used at trial. We may also send subpoenas and use other discovery mechanisms to gather additional information. It might be appropriate to conduct background checks on witnesses or defendants or send private investigators to speak with witnesses.

The next step in the process is to conduct oral depositions, which we generally do on the defendant unless the defendant has already admitted liability. We also present our client for deposition and possibly take depositions of other witnesses. During this stage in the process, we likely file a motion to enter, which essentially informs the court that we believe the case is ready to be set on the trial docket. While this does not necessarily mean the case is going to trial, it gives us the ability to set deadlines. This is important because many cases don't get settled unless there are deadlines. Nothing settles cases better than a looming trial date. We will appear in front of the judge, who will enter a scheduling order. This scheduling order sets the case for pretrial and sets deadlines for discovery, witness and exhibit lists, experts, medical examinations, and other deadlines that are necessary to keep the case moving toward a resolution.

The defense is entitled to have the plaintiff examined by a doctor of their choosing at what they like to call an "independent medical examination." The proper term for this examination is "defense medical examination" because the doctors who perform them are not independent at all. They are hired and paid by the insurance company and defense attorneys. In essence, they are hired and trained to defeat or minimize the plaintiff's case. During the defense medical examination, the most important thing to do is answer questions truthfully and accurately. We will sometimes video or audio record these medical examinations just to make sure the doctor does not misrepresent what occurred during the exam.

There may or may not be a deadline to mediate the case. We may be ordered, or we may simply agree to mediate your case. Generally speaking, mediation is beneficial in that it helps settle most cases and it allows us to identify weaknesses and strengths in the case that otherwise might go undetected. We cannot properly evaluate a case until we understand where the possible weaknesses lie. If mediation is pursued, we decide (in conjunction with the other side) who should act as the third-party mediator. Mediation can last anywhere from 10 minutes to two days, or even longer. During mediation, it is our hope we can convince the defense attorney or insurance carrier to offer the most they're willing to pay to settle the case without going to trial.

At that point, the lawyer goes through the same process they did before the case was filed (i.e., estimate the cost of taking the case to trial, discuss the risks and probable outcomes of the case and run the numbers) so the plaintiff can make a good, sound, unemotional business decision about whether or not to settle the case or proceed to trial. If the case doesn't settle at mediation, it may still settle prior to trial. However, we will continue preparations for the trial, which will include lining up doctors, getting the witnesses ready, and preparing our exhibits. This is when the case can become very expensive, which is why we try to first resolve it through mediation.

The length of time before the actual trial will occur depends on the county where it's being held. For example, in Oklahoma County, most trial dates are being scheduled four to six months from the time we request one. In other jurisdictions, we may have to wait years for a trial date. During the litigation process, we prepare to present the case in the best light and advocate for as much money as we can legally and ethically obtain. It should be noted that just because a case has been set for trial does not mean that the trial will actually occur. By simply preparing for trial, it will likely cause the insurance carrier, defense attorneys, and defendants to avoid it by paying what is necessary to resolve the case.

Does The Threat Of Going To Trial Enhance The Likelihood Of A Larger Settlement From An Insurance Company?

Insurance companies and defense attorneys know which lawyers will try a lawsuit. They watch every verdict that comes out of the state of Oklahoma. It will add significant value to your case to hire a lawyer who has a reputation for taking cases to trial when necessary. Most lawyers are scared to go to the courthouse and try a lawsuit, or they are simply too lazy. This is why you should look for a lawyer who has a history of trial experience. It is a good idea to ask a lawyer how many cases they have tried with a jury over the last 12-24 months.

Going to trial can be a risk for both parties. The plaintiff risks being compensated less than what they were initially offered or receiving zero while the defendant risks being required to pay more than what they offered. Should the case go to trial, the jurors are the ones who will decide how much the claim is worth.

How Does Going To Trial Affect The Overall Costs Of A Trucking Accident Case?

Going to trial is very expensive. On a regular run-of-the-mill case, we spend about $10,000 to $20,000 in litigation expenses. In some cases, it is common to spend hundreds of thousands to prepare a case for trial. If we decide to take a case to trial, we will spend the money that is necessary to get it ready for trial. That does not mean we will spend unnecessary amounts or that we will spend money on everything. This means the closer you get to trial, the costlier it becomes, and ultimately that is money coming out of your pocket. However, being prepared and showing the defense attorneys that you mean business and are ready for trial adds value to your case.

How Does Going To Trial Affect My Settlement?

Taking a trucking accident personal injury case to trial is expensive. There are many expenses incurred in prepping for trial such as hiring experts, paying doctors for their time, purchasing materials to support your claim, etc. Plaintiff attorneys usually work on contingency fee contracts, meaning they get a percentage of the plaintiff's settlement and get any case expenses reimbursed. If the case is lost and no settlement was recovered, the client usually doesn't owe the attorney anything, sometimes not even the costs incurred. Because the cost of going to trial is expensive, I as a plaintiff attorney run the risk of losing thousands of dollars. Ultimately, if there is a settlement, the attorney will be reimbursed for the costs advanced. Going to trial increases the costs of the case and takes your control of the case away from you.

After the motion to enter, there are pretrial motions. This is the point where the parties may file discovery motions, motions to compel, or a motion for summary judgment. Based on an issue of liability or technicality, the defendant may ask the court to dismiss the entire case. There will also be trial motions prior to trial, which include motions in limine and Daubert challenges, whereby both sides may ask the court to limit expert opinions or strike experts. The average length of the trial for a typical run-of-the-mill car wreck case is two or three days. For a complex case, it could take two weeks to try the case. Once a verdict is rendered, you will be faced with post-trial motions, such as motions for a new trial or motions to set aside or reduce the verdict. In addition, you will face the potential of an appeal.

What Happens After The Trial?

There are many things that can happen after a trial, including post-trial motions, potential motions for attorney fees, motions for costs, motions for a new trial, and motions for remittitur. Even if you lose the case, there's still a chance that the case will resolve depending on whether or not there is a potentially reversible error at the trial. If an appeal occurs, it likely takes one to two years before a decision on the appeal is rendered. It is important to note that the costs of an appeal can be very significant.

CHAPTER 13

EXPERIENCED TRUCKING ACCIDENT ATTORNEYS GET BETTER RESULTS

The biggest reason you need an attorney who is specifically experienced in handling trucking accident cases is that the trucking industry is regulated by the federal government. The federal rules associated with it come from the Federal Motor Carrier Safety Administration, and they provide countless rules associated with the trucking industry that you need to know. Depending on the facts of the case, the driver or the company might be in violation of one of those rules and regulations attributable to the trucking industry.

It's also important to know the proper people to hire and questions to ask:

- Do you need an investigator or accident reconstructionist at the scene?
- Do you need someone to take statements from the witnesses?
- Do we need to gather electronic evidence that can be destroyed or lost?
- Do you need a trucking expert to explain why the wreck occurred?

You need someone with experience to determine if the accident occurred from a simple mistake by a driver or is it a bigger issue such as a company policy. You need an attorney who knows if the wreck is the driver's fault or the company's fault. You need an attorney that has the right people and experts to hire to properly prepare your case for trial. You need any attorney that has tried a semi wreck case to a jury.

Most wrecks don't just happen because of a simple decision. If you really dig into it, it is a failure on the part of a company to make sure that these truck drivers are willing to drive. You need a lawyer that knows the trucking industry. Someone who knows how to gather the right evidence and how to look at a case to figure out the theories of recovery and liability, then apply them to the facts of the case to maximize the client's recovery. You need someone with the skill and experience to do it all in a timely, efficient, and economical manner.

We have years of experience handling trucking wreck cases in Oklahoma. We have tried numerous trucking cases to juries. There is nothing I like better than standing in front of a jury to say, "Ladies and gentlemen, I don't mind trucking companies driving through Oklahoma. In fact, I think we need them. It's a vital part of our economy. But when trucking companies drive through the state of Oklahoma, we need their company to make sure these truck drivers do it safely. They need to be properly trained, educated and provided the materials to ensure when they cross the border into Oklahoma, they do so in a safe manner that won't hurt our fellow Oklahomans."

How Much Will A Lawyer Cost?

Typical trucking accident injury cases usually cost 1/3 to 50 percent of the gross recovery, depending, on who you hire and what work was required. We typically work on a sliding scale. Meaning that the percentage goes up depending on what stage in the process we are in when the case resolves. At no time will we ever charge more than 50 percent for attorney fees. Most lawyers will offer a free initial consultation so you can get your questions answered and decide whether you want to hire that lawyer. When you're looking for or interviewing lawyers, always think about the long-term relationship you will have with that person. If you do not like your lawyer or you are not comfortable with the lawyer you are interviewing, then that is not the right attorney for you. There may be times when you don't hear from the lawyer for extended periods of time, and you must be comfortable enough to have faith that the lawyer is properly working on the case and pushing it toward a successful resolution. Look for a lawyer who is honest, hardworking, and experienced in handling cases similar to yours.

What Do You Say To Trucking Accident Victims who say, "Liability Is Clear. I Can Handle This On My Own."?

If a potential client wants to handle a matter on their own, I always tell them that that is fine and that they can call us anytime they may have questions. I will never push a person to hire our firm. However, mistakes can be made while dealing with the insurance company, and many times they will try to use your own words against you. Once a mistake has been made, it is impossible to take it back. Insurance companies try to discount certain injuries and offer clients unreasonable settlements. This is why it is important to hire an experienced professional who knows how the system works as soon as possible.

What Information Is Critical To Share With My Trucking Accident Attorney?

It is important you share as much detailed information from the incident as you can. Provide any documentation you may have, such as insurance verifications, police reports, pictures, medical records, and bills, etc. It is important you inform your attorney of the injuries you sustained and your treatment plan. Be sure to tell your attorney about any pre-existing medical issues so that they can be addressed from the beginning of your case. Insurance companies and defense attorneys will look at your past medical history to determine if your injuries are a result of the accident or if they are old injuries. That is not to say the incident didn't make your old injuries worse. As a plaintiff's attorney, we hire experts who can substantiate the cause of your current injuries.

CHAPTER 14

IF I HIRE JOE CARSON TO BE MY LAWYER, WHAT HAPPENS NEXT?

During an initial consultation, we will discuss all the details of your case. You should come prepared with all of the information pertinent to the event (e.g., medical records, incident reports, accident reports, photographs, insurance information, etc.). After a thorough review of this information, I will decide whether you have a case I can help resolve. If so, the next step would be to retain us (in Oklahoma, an attorney must receive a retainer agreement executed by the client prior to working on a case). If you decide to retain us, we will provide you with medical authorizations and other documents necessary to get your case started. Once those documents are executed, we will begin working on your case.

My office will open a file, give notice to the proper parties (including the defendant and insurance companies), and start gathering evidence. Some cases will require us to hire investigators, reconstructionists, or experts. While we do what's necessary to properly investigate the case, you will focus on getting better. If we need you, we will email, text, or call you. Should you have any questions, you can call our firm at any time or schedule an appointment to come in and see us.

Once a doctor has determined you have reached maximum medical improvement, meaning that further treatment will not improve your condition or your injuries have resolved, we will finalize the gathering of the medical records, medical bills, and other necessary documents in order to submit your claim to the insurance company. It is my belief we should usually submit a case for settlement before a lawsuit is filed in order to give the insurance company the opportunity to do what's right and settle the case. It usually takes about 60 to 90 days for an insurance company to review and make an offer on a run-of-the-mill case.

Once an offer is made in your trucking accident case, we will discuss it with you and decide how to proceed in order to make you as whole as possible. Once the negotiation process starts, we will go back and forth with the insurance company by email, letter, or telephone until we receive the highest amount, they are willing to offer. Some insurance representatives are fair and reasonable, while others are not. We will discuss the pros and cons, as well as the potential outcomes of accepting the offer versus proceeding with a lawsuit. I never tell clients what they should do. I simply give them all of the information they need in order to make an informed unemotional business decision that is right for them.

What Is It That Sets You Apart In Handling Trucking Accident Injury Cases?

Our mission at Warhawk Legal is to fight for justice by delivering exceptional legal representation to our clients through providing the highest quality guidance and support. We are a tenacious team dedicated to legal excellence in achieving outstanding results. We take pride in our commitment to delivering personalized solutions with a focus on our clients, communication, and accessibility.

What sets me apart is Integrity, Strong Work Ethic, and Reputation. These are the cornerstones of practice at Warhawk Legal. In the legal profession, you only have your reputation. I say what I do and do what I say. There is no lawyer that will outwork me. The insurance companies and defense attorneys know I will try a case when needed. If your case needs to be tried by a jury, you can expect me to do that. In my 20 years of practice, I have built a network of connections and an honorable reputation that can be beneficial to my clients in helping to achieve the highest and best result in their cases.

CHAPTER 15

FREQUENTLY ASKED QUESTIONS

Q: If I Have Been Injured in a Trucking Accident Does That Mean I Am Automatically Going to Receive Money?

Because you have been injured in a trucking accident does not mean you automatically receive money damages. What you do have the right to do is (1) make a claim and (2) have an opportunity to prove by admissible evidence the incident was caused by the negligence of others and that the negligence was the direct cause of the injuries and damages you sustained.

Q: When Should I Hire A Trucking Accident Lawyer After A Wreck?

For "fender benders" and routine car accident claims with no personal injuries, you may not need to hire a lawyer. However, if you have been seriously injured in a trucking accident, you should hire an attorney immediately.

Here are a few things to think about before deciding whether or not you should try to handle your own claim:

1: Is Fault Contested In Your Case Or Does The Truck Driver And Insurance Company Admit Fault?

If there is a dispute over who caused the accident and you cannot prove the other driver is at fault, it may be best to retain an attorney. The stakes could be high, and you could recover nothing.

2: How Much Are Your Out-Of-Pocket Expenses For Medical Bills And Lost Wages?

You must decide at what point your case is too big to handle yourself and when it is time to hire a lawyer.

3: How Badly Were You Injured And How Long Did It Take You To Recover?

If you have a serious injury or one that is permanent, you have a potentially large claim and should hire a lawyer who can present it in a professional manner.

4: Are You Going To Court?

If you are unable to resolve the situation outside of court, it is a good idea to hire a lawyer who knows the rules, can protect your legal rights, and give you a fighting chance at winning.

5: How Much Time Do You Want To Devote To The Case?

These types of cases can be confusing, time consuming, and costly. You are better off spending your time doing something you like to do or earning a living and letting someone else that handles these types of cases worry about your case.

Q: How Long Should I Wait Before Contacting A Trucking Accident Lawyer?

The sooner an experienced trucking accident can get started working for you the better. Remember, in almost every situation when you are injured or have property damage, you have only a certain amount of time to file a claim. The longer you wait, the more difficult it may be to obtain the evidence you need to support your case. Furthermore, if you have submitted your claim to an insurance company, the insurance adjuster you are dealing with may have settled hundreds of cases in the past year alone. He or she is highly trained at negotiation. It is important to be very cautious in talking with an insurance adjuster; they are trained to save the insurance company money. If they can beat your case, they will try. They will use your own words against you. Be careful what you say to the trained professionals.

Q: What Documentation Should I Bring When I Meet With A Lawyer?

The more information you can provide, the easier it will be for an attorney to determine if your claim will be successful. You should supply any documents that may have a bearing on your case. Be overly prepared when deciding what to bring to your initial meeting with your attorney. While the documents you need to bring depends on the nature of the case, it is generally a good idea to bring any papers relating to the incident or the parties involved. Lawsuit papers, incident reports, photographs, medical records, medical bills, written statements, repair estimates, and invoices are all examples of items that may be important to your case and will need to be shown to your lawyer. Information about the other driver's insurance is extremely helpful. It is also a prudent idea to bring a list of the names and contact information of anyone involved with the incident as well as all witness information. Prior to the first meeting, doing a timeline of important events relating to the incident can be helpful in terms of jogging your memory and assisting the attorney in understanding when and how things occurred. Remember, it's better to be over prepared than under prepared. If you haven't collected any documents prior to meeting with a lawyer, do not worry. The lawyer will be able to direct you in the right direction in obtaining the documents you may need.

Q: What Can I Expect At The Initial Consultation?

You will be asked to complete some simple intake forms much like going to a doctor's office. Most of the time the lawyer should be able to tell you whether you have a legal claim that has merit. If it does, you should discuss the terms of the lawyer's representation. If you have decided to choose that particular lawyer, he, or she may ask you to sign a retainer agreement. A lawyer cannot represent you without a written retainer agreement. Once that agreement has been signed, your attorney will then start gathering information he or she will need to try your case. No competent lawyer should tell you what your case is worth at the first visit. To arrive at a figure for damages, your lawyer will need to examine the extent of your injuries, your pain and suffering, disability, disfigurement, the cost of medical treatment, and lost wages.

Q: What Are The Benefits Of Hiring A Lawyer?

Unfortunately, accidents involving semi-trucks happen every day. Some result in minor vehicle damage and can generally be handled alone by contacting the insurance company. However, accidents involving physical injury, fatality, or other significant damage may warrant the legal representation of an experienced trucking accident injury attorney. Many times, in these types of serious accidents, you can sustain injuries that don't manifest themselves until later. If you settle with your insurance company, you may realize in the future that what you settled for didn't properly consider future complications. While certain matters, such as a minor fender bender, may not require an attorney's help, there are many instances where retaining an attorney would be beneficial to your case. First of all, a lawyer is able to navigate the complexities of the law as well as the legal jargon that may stump you and cause you to misinterpret the situation thereby hindering your case. Having a lawyer on your side can help you avoid problems, as opposed to fixing them once they arise. Money is almost always a consideration for potential clients, so it is important to note that hiring an attorney can actually save you money. In fact, most lawyers provide a free initial consultation and many civil lawyers do not collect a dime unless they win your case. Remember an experienced lawyer has probably seen cases similar to yours or at least knows enough to make an educated guess about how it might resolve. Sometimes a settlement is the best choice, and an attorney can help you fairly negotiate with the opposing party. Most importantly, a lawyer should be able to take some of the burden and stress of handling a case from you and will ensure your case is properly handled.

Q: What Will You Do For Me If I Hire You?

Our firm will make every effort to settle your trucking accident claim without the necessity of litigation. Initially, we will notify the person or entity that may be at fault, as well as their insurance company. At that time, we will begin investigating the claim and preparing it to submit to the insurance companies. The insurance companies will also be investigating the claim. During this time, we may ask for periodic medical reports so we can follow the progress of your medical treatment. You may also be asked to give a statement to us, an insurance adjuster, or an attorney for the insurance company concerning the facts surrounding your claim. An attorney with our firm will be with you if you are required to give a statement, and we will explain this to you in further detail if your statement is necessary.

Q: How Long Will My Case Take?

BE PATIENT. The legal process has a pace of its own and cannot be hurried. Your case will not be submitted for settlement until it is ready for settlement. That does not mean that we will not be doing anything. In fact, we will be getting it ready to submit. Cases like yours are many times affected by events outside the control of any attorney. Possible delays in the resolution of your case are too many to list but include things such as delayed medical treatment, failure of a client in communicating with the attorney, sickness of a party or adjuster, judge being out of town, and failure of an insurance company to conduct a meaningful and timely investigation. The more complex your case, the longer it will likely take to get it resolved. We want to get your case resolved as soon as possible and will pursue your claim with diligence. Generally, it is our desire to move your case as quickly as possible. However, sometimes the wisest course is not always the fastest. Remember, we don't get paid until you get paid.

Q: How Do I Pay A Lawyer For My Trucking Accident Case?

When you hire our firm for your truck wreck injury case, you will pay for the attorney fees only if you recover funds for your injuries. This is called a contingency fee agreement. The percentage paid to the attorney will differ based on the type of case, as well as the complexity of the case, and the probability of success. For example, for a complex and/or difficult case, the attorney might charge 50% while for a simple car wreck case, the attorney might only charge 1/3 of the recovery.

It is important to note that costs are different than fees. For example, when you hire our firm, we will incur costs associated with your case. We will have to pay for things such as filing fees, medical records, and police reports, as well as postage, copies, experts, investigators, etc. Every firm treats costs differently. We will usually front most costs and be paid back at the time of settlement from the client's portion of the settlement.

Q: If I Hire A Lawyer Does That Mean I Have To Go To Trial?

Not necessarily. The majority of cases resolve themselves prior to trial. Ultimately, the decision to go to trial will be yours. We will never tell you that you have to go to trial. We will tell you the pros and cons, as well as the risks and potential rewards of proceeding to trial. The ultimate decision as to whether or not you go to trial is yours and yours alone.

Q: Why Would My Case Go To Trial?

Your truck accident case would go to trial because you choose to go to trial, and the insurance company has not made an acceptable settlement offer. You will be given all of the necessary information to make this decision. Your attorney will be available to answer any questions you may have before you make the decision. It should be noted that your attorney may not take a case to trial or may advise against going to trial if it has been determined that it is not economically feasible to do so.

Q: Why Isn't The Insurance Company Simply Being Fair?

The insurance company is not in the business of insurance to be fair and pay claims. The more money the insurance company pays out, the less money the insurance company makes.

Q: If I Decide To Go To Trial, Do I Get To Sue The Insurance Carrier?

In most situations, you are prohibited by the laws of the State of Oklahoma from naming an insurance carrier as a party Defendant. You must sue the responsible party, not their insurance carrier. In fact, in Oklahoma you are prohibited from even mentioning insurance at trial. If you mention insurance at trial, it is possible a judge will grant a mistrial and you could be responsible for the other side's attorney fees and costs. The Oklahoma legislature has said that whether or not a person carries insurance is not relevant to the facts of the case. This hurts the Plaintiff in most situations. For example, the jury may feel sorry for the Defendant thinking the Defendant has to pay out of their own pocket. In most circumstances, a Defendant will never have to pay anything. In fact, if a Plaintiff gets an excess verdict, over and above a Defendants insurance policy, it is likely that the Defendant's insurance carrier will pay the entire verdict even if the judgment is more than the policy limits of the Defendant.

Q: If We Go To Trial, Will The Jury Know That There Is Insurance To Pay The Verdict?

Probably not. In most cases in Oklahoma, a jury is not permitted to hear whether or not the defendant has insurance. Insurance companies have done an excellent job of lobbying our legislature and getting judges to rule insurance is not relevant at trial. Hardly ever does a Defendant have to pay money out of their own pocket. However, the jury is not privy to this information. The jury for all we know believes that the Defendant has to pay this money out of his or her own pocket. That is not so. We would hardly ever consider taking a case to trial unless there was insurance. The reasons for that are because of the time, effort, and expense it takes to take a case to trial. We have to weigh whether or not there is a chance or a likelihood, that we will recover those costs, attorney fees, and expenses. If there is no insurance, it is more likely than not that all of the time and expense put into a case would never be recouped. Rarely would a Defendant have to pay anything out of their own pocket. In fact, if a Defendant ever has to pay something out of his own pocket, it is quite possible they may have a lawsuit against their own insurance carrier for what is called bad faith, for not settling the case within their policy limits.

Q: What If My Health Insurance Carrier Has Paid My Medical Expenses? What Happens Then?

If you collect money from the Defendant, you may have to pay your health insurance carrier back.

Q: Who Hires The Lawyer That Represents The Defendant?

The Defendant's insurance carrier pays for the lawyer representing the Defendant. Sometimes the lawyer representing the Defendant is even an employee of the Defendant's insurance carrier. The jury will never know this information. The jury is likely to believe the Defendant is paying for that lawyer out of his own pocket. This is not so. In all reality, the Defendant is not charged anything for his defense.

Q: How Much Will It Cost To Take My Case To Trial?

Thousands and thousands of dollars. The type of case it is, and the complexity of the case determines how much it will cost to take your case to trial. If your case is a simple rear end collision car wreck case, it is likely we will spend somewhere in the neighborhood of $10,000-$20,000 preparing your case for trial. If your case is a trucking wreck, product liability, medical malpractice, or complex case, it is likely we will spend an excess of $150,000-$200,000 preparing your case for trial.

Q: Who Is The Doctor The Defendant Uses At Trial?

More likely than not, it will be a doctor who has been hired by the insurance company or the defense attorney many times in the past. There are certain doctors that are hired to perform these functions. Most doctors will not do this type of work since they are usually busy helping patients and do not have the time. These defense doctors make a living by writing reports for the insurance company helping them attempt to reduce the amount of money the insurance company has to pay a Plaintiff. These doctors are biased and prejudiced and will say whatever it takes in order to win a case. They are hired to render "opinions." Remember, a doctor can have an opinion that makes no sense at all. Even if he is wrong, it is just his opinion. They are professional testifiers, and they can handle the courtroom. They have testified hundreds and thousands of times across the state of Oklahoma, and they get paid to minimize the amount the insurance company has to pay a Plaintiff.

Q: What Is A Deposition?

A deposition is a statement given under oath, usually taken in a lawyer's office or a court reporting firm before a court reporter. Witnesses are called to testify in a deposition and answer questions posed by the attorneys representing both parties in a case. The court reporter produces a written transcript of everything said at the deposition, and the witnesses read and sign the transcript swearing it to be an accurate statement of the evidence given under oath.

Q: What Should I Wear To Depositions, Court, or Mediation?

People commonly ask me what they should wear during depositions, mediation, or court proceedings, and I simply say wear what's comfortable. You want to look presentable and respectable, but you don't need to dress up as if you're going to a wedding or church. What I might recommend to one person would possibly make another person uncomfortable. I would suggest dressing as if you were going to a job interview. Some people wear jeans and a nice shirt and others wear a suit and tie. The main thing is we want you comfortable. Always know that people are watching and judging you, whether it be the mediator, opposing counsel, or jury. First impressions matter, so try to make a good one.

Q: What Is A Contingent Fee?

A fee is contingent when it is conditioned upon your attorney's successful resolution of your case. It is often referred to as: "No fee unless you win." However, the client is generally responsible for the "out-of-pocket" costs of litigation (which most of the time will be waived if the case is lost). A Contingent Fee is paid as a percentage of your monetary recovery.

Q: Should I Provide A Statement To An Insurance Company Without Help From a Lawyer?

No. The more significant your injuries, the more important it is to seek legal counsel before talking to an insurance company. The insurance company may try to diminish the significance of your injuries or talk you into taking a settlement below what you deserve. It would be detrimental to provide an incomplete statement early in the process until you and your attorney know the details and severity of your injuries. You should have your attorney present if you give a statement to an insurance adjuster or lawyer for the insurance company. This will ensure you are properly protected and there are no improper questions asked.

Q: Do I Have A Case If I Do Not Feel Hurt?

You may still have a case even if you do not feel hurt at the scene. The biological response to a traumatic situation like an accident sends a rush of adrenaline through the body, which can temporarily reduce sensations of pain. You may start feeling significant pain or developing other symptoms hours or days after the wreck. It is wise to consult a doctor even if you do not feel immediate, excruciating pain, since some of the most serious conditions emerge over time; sometimes, even days or weeks after an event.

Q: What Should I Do If An Adjuster From The "At-Fault" Driver's Insurance Company Calls Me?

Do not speak with the adjuster. Refer the adjuster to your attorney. Also, do not speak with the attorney for the "at-fault" driver. These are highly trained individuals who are trying to speak with you to either beat your case or minimize what their employer has to pay you. They may even be recording you without your knowledge.

Q: How Long Will It Take To Settle My Claim?

There is no set answer to this question. All cases are different. The more complex the case, the longer it usually takes to settle. If you have substantial injuries, the longer it will take. The more money there is at stake for the insurance company, the longer it will take. In most cases, the settlement process starts when your doctor releases you from treatment. Assuming your attorney has all of your accident-related records, your claim could be filed with the insurance company in five to ten business days. It may take the adjuster four to six weeks to evaluate your claim and make an initial offer. At this point, it's a matter of both sides negotiating a dollar amount that is reasonable for your case and acceptable to you. If you receive medical treatment for two to four months, it is possible your claim could be settled within six months. Most of the time, for a simple clear liability case, it will take between 6 to 12 months to settle your case. However, if the case is more complex, or if there are disputes as to liability or damages, it could take years to complete your case.

Q: Is It Okay To Post Things About My Case On Social Media?

Do not post anything about your case on social media (Facebook, Twitter, Instagram, etc.). Many cases have been lost, or severely damaged, as a result of a client posting or saying something trying to be funny or simply not understanding how a defense attorney would twist their statements or intent. I advise all clients to be very careful with what they post and to enable their privacy settings. Before you post something ask yourself whether or not it would embarrass you if it were posted on the front page of the local paper. Another example of how this can hurt you is if you claim to be injured as a result of your claim and you post a picture of yourself doing a handstand, water skiing, running a marathon, etc. Photos like these will ultimately kill your case.

Q: Is There Ever A Guarantee I Will Win My Case?

There are never any guarantees you will win or lose your claim. We cannot and will not guarantee the result we achieve will be the result you may desire. There is no way to predict what a jury will do when it makes its decision. The laws concerning most cases are written in a manner where a jury can do whatever it believes is right. The question then becomes what will a jury think is right? No one can predict what a jury thinks is right. The only promises we can give you are that we will work hard for you, be honest with you, and properly prepare your case. To predict what a judge or jury may do with your case is virtually impossible.

APPENDIX I

2019 Traffic Safety Report by US DOT National Highway Traffic Safety Administration

May 2021

DOT HS 813 110

NHTSA

In this fact sheet for 2019 the information is presented as follows.

- Overview
- Crash Characteristics
- Drivers
- State

Large Trucks

A large truck as defined in this fact sheet is any medium or heavy truck, excluding buses and motor homes, with a gross vehicle weight rating (GVWR) greater than 10,000 pounds. These large trucks include both commercial and non-commercial vehicles. In 2019 seventy-five percent of the large trucks involved in fatal traffic crashes were heavy large trucks (GVWR > 26,000 lbs.).

Key Findings

- In 2019 there were 5,005 people killed in crashes involving large trucks. This number was almost the same as in 2018 (5,006).
- Seventy-one percent of people killed in large-truck crashes in 2019 were occupants of other vehicles.
- Seventy-seven percent of the fatal crashes involving large trucks in 2019 occurred on weekdays (6 a.m. Monday to 5:59 p.m. Friday).
- Two percent of the drivers of large trucks involved in fatal crashes in 2019 had blood alcohol concentrations (BACs) of .08 grams per deciliter (g/dL) or higher, much lower than drivers of other vehicle types (29% for motorcycles, 20% for passenger cars, and 19% for light trucks).
- In 2019 drivers of large trucks in fatal crashes were less likely than drivers of passenger cars to have previous license suspensions or revocations.
- Large-truck drivers involved in fatal crashes in 2019 had a higher percentage (22.9%) of previously recorded crashes compared to drivers of other vehicle types (motorcycles, 22.0%; passenger cars, 18.9%; and light trucks, 17.8%).

This fact sheet contains information on fatal motor vehicle traffic crashes based on data from the Fatality Analysis Reporting System (FARS) and non-fatal motor vehicle traffic crashes from the National Automotive Sampling System (NASS) General Estimates System (GES) and Crash Report Sampling System (CRSS). Refer to the end of this publication for more information on FARS, NASS GES, and CRSS.

A motor vehicle traffic crash is defined as an incident that involved one or more motor vehicles in transport that originated on a public trafficway, such as a road or highway. Crashes that occurred on private property, including parking lots and driveways, are excluded. The terms "motor vehicle traffic crash" and "traffic crash" are used interchangeably.

U.S. Department of Transportation
National Highway Traffic Safety Administration
1200 New Jersey Avenue SE
Washington, DC 20590

NHTSA's National Center for Statistics and Analysis

Overview

In 2019 there were 5,005 people killed and an estimated 159,000 people injured in crashes involving large trucks. An estimated 538,000 large trucks were involved in police-reported traffic crashes nationwide during 2019.

Table 1 provides an overview of people killed and injured in crashes involving large trucks from 2010 to 2019.

Fatalities in crashes involving large trucks increased by 2 percent from 2017 to 2018, and remained relatively the same from 2018 to 2019. Of the fatalities in 2019:

- 71 percent (3,544) were occupants of other vehicles;
- 18 percent (892) were occupants of large trucks; and
- 11 percent (569) were nonoccupants (pedestrians, pedalcyclists, etc.).

From 2018 to 2019 there was a 1-percent decrease in the number of occupants of other vehicles killed, and a 3-percent increase in the number of nonoccupants killed. This is the highest number of nonoccupants killed in the most recent 10-year period (2010 to 2019), and the second highest number of occupants of other vehicles killed in that 10-year period.

In 2019 there were an estimated 159,000 people injured in crashes involving large trucks—an increase of 5 percent from an estimated 151,000 in 2018. Of the people injured in 2019:

- 69 percent (110,000) were occupants of other vehicles;
- 29 percent (46,000) were occupants of large trucks; and
- 3 percent (4,000) were nonoccupants (pedestrians, pedalcyclists, etc.).

From 2018 to 2019 there was a 17-percent increase in the number of injured large-truck occupants in large-truck crashes, and a 19-percent increase in the number of nonoccupants injured. There was a 1-percent increase in the number of occupants of other vehicles injured in those same crashes.

Table 1

People Killed and Injured in Crashes Involving Large Trucks, by Person Type and Crash Type, 2010–2019

	Truck Occupants by Crash Type						Other People						
	Single Vehicle		Multiple Vehicle		Total		Occupants of Other Vehicles		Nonoccupants		Total		
Year	Number	Percent	Number	Percent	Number	Percent	Number	Percent	Number	Percent	Number	Percent	Total
							Killed						
2010	339	9%	191	5%	530	14%	2,797	76%	359	10%	3,156	86%	3,686
2011	408	11%	232	6%	640	17%	2,713	72%	428	11%	3,141	83%	3,781
2012	423	11%	274	7%	697	18%	2,857	72%	390	10%	3,247	82%	3,944
2013	431	11%	264	7%	695	17%	2,845	71%	441	11%	3,286	83%	3,981
2014	405	10%	251	6%	656	17%	2,859	73%	393	10%	3,252	83%	3,908
2015	395	10%	270	7%	665	16%	3,017	74%	413	10%	3,430	84%	4,095
2016	520	11%	295	6%	815	17%	3,351	72%	512	11%	3,863	83%	4,678
2017	525	11%	353	7%	878	18%	3,535	72%	493	10%	4,028	82%	4,906
2018	538	11%	352	7%	890	18%	3,563	71%	553	11%	4,116	82%	5,006
2019	495	10%	397	8%	892	18%	3,544	71%	569	11%	4,113	82%	5,005
							Injured						
2010	9,000	11%	11,000	13%	20,000	25%	59,000	73%	2,000	2%	61,000	75%	81,000
2011	7,000	8%	16,000	17%	23,000	26%	64,000	72%	2,000	2%	66,000	74%	89,000
2012	9,000	9%	16,000	16%	25,000	24%	76,000	73%	3,000	3%	79,000	76%	104,000
2013	9,000	9%	16,000	16%	25,000	26%	69,000	72%	2,000	2%	71,000	74%	96,000
2014	10,000	9%	17,000	15%	27,000	24%	82,000	74%	2,000	2%	85,000	76%	112,000
2015	10,000	9%	20,000	17%	30,000	26%	85,000	72%	3,000	2%	88,000	74%	118,000
2016†	13,000	10%	23,000	17%	36,000	27%	95,000	70%	4,000	3%	99,000	73%	135,000
2017†	15,000	10%	25,000	17%	40,000	27%	106,000	71%	3,000	2%	108,000	73%	148,000
2018†	13,000	9%	26,000	17%	39,000	26%	108,000	72%	3,000	2%	112,000	74%	151,000
2019†	15,000	10%	30,000	19%	46,000	29%	110,000	69%	4,000	3%	114,000	71%	159,000

Sources: FARS 2010–2018 Final File, 2019 Annual Report File (ARF); NASS GES 2010–2015; CRSS 2016–2019

†CRSS estimates and NASS GES estimates are not comparable due to different sample designs. Refer to end of document for more information about CRSS.

Note: Injury totals may not equal sum of components due to independent rounding.

In 2019 large trucks accounted for 10 percent of all vehicles involved in fatal crashes and 4 percent of all vehicles involved in injury and property-damage-only crashes. Large trucks accounted for 4 percent of all registered vehicles and 9 percent of the total vehicle miles traveled (VMT) in 2019. In comparison, passenger vehicles (passenger cars, SUVs, pickup trucks, and vans) accounted for 92 percent of all registered vehicles and 90 percent of the total VMT in 2019.

Table 2 summarizes the number of large trucks involved in fatal and injury crashes, the number of registered large trucks, involvement rates for every 100,000 registered large trucks, large-truck VMT, and the involvement rates for every 100 million large-truck VMT from 2010 to 2019.

Table 2

Large Trucks Involved in Fatal and Injury Crashes, and Involvement Rates, 2010–2019

Year	Number of Large Trucks Involved	Number of Large Trucks Registered	Involvement Rate per 100,000 Registered Large Trucks	Large-Truck VMT (millions)	Involvement Rate per 100 Million Large-Truck VMT
			Fatal Crashes		
2010	3,494	10,770,054	32.44	286,527	1.22
2011	3,633	10,270,693	35.37	267,594	1.36
2012	3,825	10,659,380	35.88	269,207	1.42
2013	3,921	10,597,356	37.00	275,017	1.43
2014	3,749	10,905,956	34.38	279,132	1.34
2015	4,075	11,203,184	36.37	279,844	1.46
2016	4,562	11,498,561	39.67	287,895	1.58
2017	4,805	12,229,216	39.29	297,593	1.61
2018	4,909	13,233,910	37.09	304,864	1.61
2019	5,005	13,085,643	38.25	300,050	1.67
			Injury Crashes		
2010	58,000	10,770,054	541	286,527	20
2011	63,000	10,270,693	609	267,594	23
2012	77,000	10,659,380	719	269,207	28
2013	73,000	10,597,356	690	275,017	27
2014	88,000	10,905,956	811	279,132	32
2015	87,000	11,203,184	779	279,844	31
2016†	102,000	11,498,561	888	287,895	35
2017†	107,000	12,229,216	873	297,593	36
2018†	112,000	13,233,910	848	304,864	37
2019†	119,000	13,085,643	906	300,050	40

Sources: FARS 2010–2018 Final File, 2019 ARF; NASS GES 2010–2015; CRSS 2016–2019; VMT and Registered Vehicles - Federal Highway Administration

†CRSS estimates and NASS GES estimates are not comparable due to different sample designs. Refer to end of document for more information about CRSS.

Crash Characteristics

In 2019 large trucks were more likely to be involved in fatal multiple-vehicle crashes as opposed to fatal single-vehicle crashes than were passenger vehicles. Eighty-one percent of large trucks involved in fatal crashes were in multiple-vehicle crashes, compared with 62 percent for passenger vehicles.

Table 3 presents percentages of two-vehicle fatal crashes involving large trucks by initial impact point of the large truck and the other vehicle in 2019. The large truck and the other vehicle were both struck on the front of the vehicle 31 percent of the time. The large trucks were struck in the rear almost 4 times more often than the other vehicles (23% and 6%, respectively).

Table 3

Percentage of Two-Vehicle Fatal Crashes Involving Large Trucks, by Initial Impact Point, 2019

Impact Point on Large Truck	Impact Point on Other Vehicle				
	Front	Left Side	Right Side	Rear	Total
Front	31%	14%	10%	6%	**61%**
Left Side	8%	1%	0%	0%	**10%**
Right Side	6%	1%	0%	0%	**7%**
Rear	22%	0%	1%	0%	**23%**
Total	**68%**	**16%**	**11%**	**6%**	**100%**

Source: FARS 2019 ARF

Note: Totals may not equal sum of components due to independent rounding.

According to FARS data in Table 4, both the large truck and the other vehicle were proceeding straight at the time of the crash in 41 percent of the two-vehicle fatal crashes. In 10 percent of these two-vehicle crashes, the other vehicle was turning left regardless of the large-truck maneuver. In 10 percent of these crashes the truck and the other vehicle were navigating a curve. In 8 percent of the two-vehicle fatal crashes, either the truck or the other vehicle was stopped in a traffic lane (7% and 1%, respectively).

Table 4

Percentage of Vehicle Maneuvers in Two-Vehicle Fatal Crashes Involving a Large Truck, by Maneuver of the Large Truck and Maneuver of the Other Vehicle, 2019

Vehicle Maneuver of the Large Truck	Vehicle Maneuver of the Other Vehicle						Total
	Going Straight	Stopped in Road	Turning Right	Turning Left	Negotiating a Curve	Other/Unknown Maneuver	
Going Straight	41%	1%	1%	8%	1%	9%	61%
Stopped in Road	6%	–	0%	0%	0%	1%	7%
Turning Right	1%	–	–	–	–	0%	1%
Turning Left	6%	0%	–	0%	1%	1%	8%
Negotiating a Curve	1%	0%	0%	1%	10%	1%	13%
Other/Unknown Maneuver	8%	0%	0%	0%	1%	1%	10%
Total	**63%**	**1%**	**1%**	**10%**	**12%**	**13%**	**100%**

Source: FARS 2019 ARF
Note: Totals may not equal sum of components due to independent rounding.

Figure 1 shows the percentages of fatal crashes involving large trucks by roadway, urban/rural land use, work zone, day of the week (weekday/weekend), and time of day (nighttime/daytime) in 2019.

- One out of 4 fatal large-truck crashes (25%) occurred on interstates.
- Fifty-seven percent of fatal crashes involving large trucks occurred in rural areas.
- Only 6 percent of fatal crashes involving large trucks occurred in work zones.
- Seventy-seven percent of the fatal crashes involving large trucks occurred on weekdays.
- Of those large-truck fatal crashes during weekdays, 72 percent occurred during the daytime hours from 6 a.m. to 5:59 p.m.

Figure 1

Percentage of Fatal Crashes Involving Large Trucks in Relation to Roadway, Land Use, Work Zone, Day of Week and Time of Day, 2019

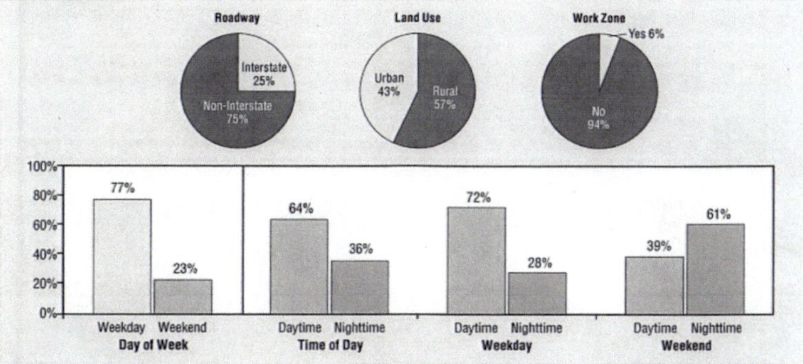

Source: FARS 2019 ARF
Note: Unknowns were removed before calculating percentages.

Weekday – Monday 6 a.m. to Friday 5:59 p.m.
Weekend – Friday 6 p.m. to Monday 5:59 a.m.

Daytime – 6 a.m. to 5:59 p.m.
Nighttime – 6 p.m. to 5:59 a.m.

Drivers

Drivers are considered to be alcohol-impaired when their BACs are .08 g/dL or higher. Figure 2 displays the proportions of alcohol-impaired drivers in fatal crashes by vehicle types (large trucks, passenger cars, light trucks, and motorcycles) over the last 10 years. The percentage of large-truck drivers involved in fatal crashes who were alcohol-impaired was 2 percent in 2019. For drivers of other types of vehicles involved in fatal crashes in 2019, the percentages of alcohol-impaired drivers were 29 percent for motorcycles, 20 percent for passenger cars, and 19 percent for light trucks.

Figure 2
Estimated Proportions of Alcohol-Impaired Drivers in Fatal Crashes, by Vehicle Type, 2010–2019

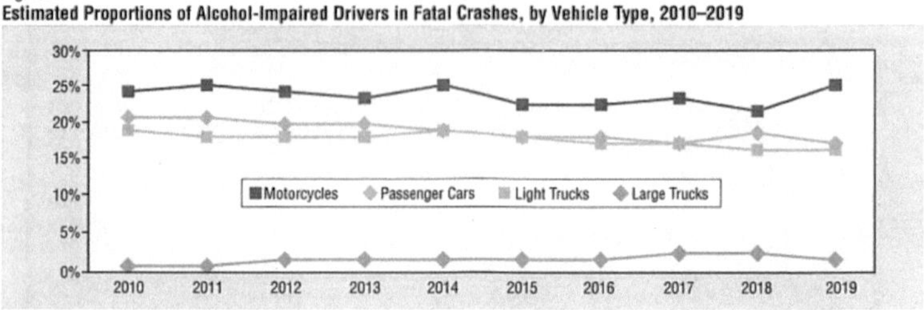

Source: FARS 2010–2018 Final File, FARS 2019 ARF

Figure 3 presents the percentages of drivers involved in fatal crashes who had previous driving records (recorded crashes, DWI convictions, speeding convictions, and recorded suspensions or revocations) within 5 years from the time of the crash, by vehicle types (motorcycles, passenger cars, light trucks, and large trucks) in 2019.

- Large-truck drivers have a higher percentage (22.9%) of previously recorded crashes compared to drivers of other vehicle types (motorcycles, 22.0%; passenger cars, 18.9%; and light trucks, 17.8%).
- Almost 20 percent of all large-truck drivers involved in fatal crashes had at least one prior speeding conviction, slightly higher than passenger car drivers (19.9% vs 18.8%) involved in fatal crashes.
- Drivers of large trucks in fatal crashes were less likely to have previous license suspensions or revocations than were passenger car drivers (8.8% and 15.4%, respectively).
- Large-truck drivers had the lowest percentage (1.0%) of previous DWI convictions compared to drivers of other vehicle types (motorcycles, 4.6%; passenger cars, 3.1%; and light trucks, 3.2%).

Figure 3
Previous 5-Year Driving Records of Drivers Involved in Fatal Crashes, by Vehicle Type, 2019

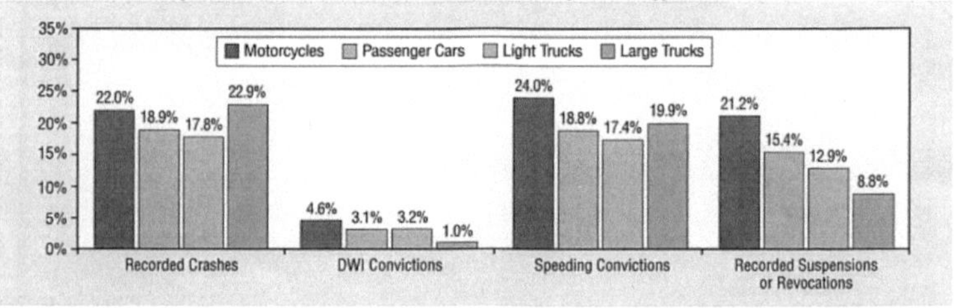

Source: FARS 2019 ARF
Note: Excludes all drivers with previous records that were unknown.

State

Figure 4 is a map that displays the percentages of large trucks involved in fatal crashes by State. Table 5 presents the large-truck involvement in fatal crashes in 2019 for the 50 States, the District of Columbia, and Puerto Rico. Puerto Rico is not included in the overall U.S. total.

- On average nationwide, 9.8 percent of all vehicles involved in fatal crashes were large trucks.
- The percentage of large trucks involved in fatal crashes, as a proportion of all vehicles, ranged from 2.0 percent in Hawaii to 25.0 percent in Wyoming. There were no large trucks involved in fatal crashes in the District of Columbia.
- The percentage of large trucks involved in fatal crashes was 10 percent or higher in 26 States.
- Texas had the highest number of large trucks involved in fatal crashes at 658, and the largest number of total vehicles involved in fatal crashes.
- The States with the higher percentages of large trucks involved in fatal crashes are in the middle of the country as compared to the eastern and western portions of the country.

Table 6 shows the number of people killed in large-truck crashes for each of the 50 States, the District of Columbia, and Puerto Rico, by person type in 2019. Puerto Rico is not included in the overall U.S. total.

- The highest number of occupants of large trucks killed was 146 in Texas, followed by 56 in California.
- The number of occupants of other vehicles killed ranged from 3 in Hawaii and Rhode Island to 433 in Texas. Ten States each had more than 100 occupants of other vehicles killed in large-truck crashes.
- Texas had the highest number of nonoccupants killed in large-truck crashes at 73. Three other States (California, Florida, New York) had 50 or more nonoccupants killed in large-truck crashes.

Additional data visualization tools for fact sheets can be found at https://cdan.dot.gov/DataVisualization/DataVisualization.htm#

Figure 4
Percentage of Large Trucks Involved in Fatal Crashes, by State, 2019

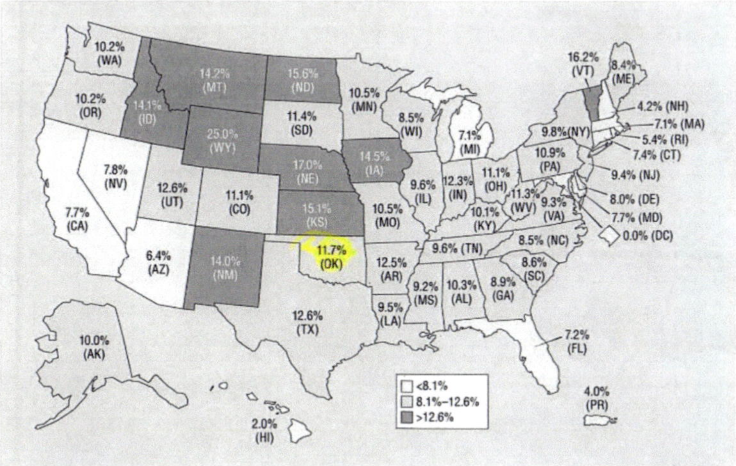

Source: FARS 2019 ARF

Table 5

Large Trucks Involved in Fatal Crashes, by State, 2019

State	Total Vehicles Involved in Fatal Crashes	Large Trucks Involved in Fatal Crashes		
		Number	Percentage of Total Vehicles	Percentage of U.S. Total for Large Trucks
Alabama	1,316	136	10.3%	2.7%
Alaska	90	9	10.0%	0.2%
Arizona	1,356	87	6.4%	1.7%
Arkansas	705	88	12.5%	1.8%
California	5,029	385	7.7%	7.7%
Colorado	870	97	11.1%	1.9%
Connecticut	339	25	7.4%	0.5%
Delaware	187	15	8.0%	0.3%
District of Columbia	34	0	0.0%	0.0%
Florida	4,745	340	7.2%	6.8%
Georgia	2,197	195	8.9%	3.9%
Hawaii	147	3	2.0%	0.1%
Idaho	305	43	14.1%	0.9%
Illinois	1,462	141	9.6%	2.8%
Indiana	1,210	149	12.3%	3.0%
Iowa	470	68	14.5%	1.4%
Kansas	551	83	15.1%	1.7%
Kentucky	1,056	107	10.1%	2.1%
Louisiana	1,022	97	9.5%	1.9%
Maine	191	16	8.4%	0.3%
Maryland	765	59	7.7%	1.2%
Massachusetts	453	32	7.1%	0.6%
Michigan	1,409	100	7.1%	2.0%
Minnesota	523	55	10.5%	1.1%
Mississippi	849	78	9.2%	1.6%
Missouri	1,236	130	10.5%	2.6%
Montana	219	31	14.2%	0.6%
Nebraska	352	60	17.0%	1.2%
Nevada	462	36	7.8%	0.7%
New Hampshire	144	6	4.2%	0.1%
New Jersey	779	73	9.4%	1.5%
New Mexico	564	79	14.0%	1.6%
New York	1,218	119	9.8%	2.4%
North Carolina	1,950	166	8.5%	3.3%
North Dakota	128	20	15.6%	0.4%
Ohio	1,661	184	11.1%	3.7%
Oklahoma	888	104	11.7%	2.1%
Oregon	655	67	10.2%	1.3%
Pennsylvania	1,616	176	10.9%	3.5%
Rhode Island	74	4	5.4%	0.1%
South Carolina	1,397	120	8.6%	2.4%
South Dakota	132	15	11.4%	0.3%
Tennessee	1,607	154	9.6%	3.1%
Texas	5,208	658	12.6%	13.1%
Utah	350	44	12.6%	0.9%
Vermont	68	11	16.2%	0.2%
Virginia	1,139	106	9.3%	2.1%
Washington	784	80	10.2%	1.6%
West Virginia	355	40	11.3%	0.8%
Wisconsin	796	68	8.5%	1.4%
Wyoming	184	46	25.0%	0.9%
U.S. Total	**51,247**	**5,005**	**9.8%**	**100.0%**
Puerto Rico	378	15	4.0%	100.0%

Source: FARS 2019 ARF

Note: Percentages may not equal sum of components due to independent rounding.

Table 6

Fatalities in Traffic Crashes Involving Large Trucks, by State and Person Type, 2019

State	Truck Occupants by Crash Type			Other People			Total
	Single Vehicle	Multiple Vehicle	Total	Occupants of Other Vehicles	Nonoccupants	Total	
Alabama	12	8	20	107	10	117	137
Alaska	3	0	3	5	1	6	9
Arizona	5	7	12	69	6	75	87
Arkansas	8	7	15	63	4	67	82
California	29	27	56	287	65	352	408
Colorado	11	9	20	77	6	83	103
Connecticut	3	2	5	14	2	16	21
Delaware	0	1	1	15	0	15	16
District of Columbia	0	0	0	0	0	0	0
Florida	20	32	52	241	56	297	349
Georgia	20	11	31	161	12	173	204
Hawaii	0	0	0	3	0	3	3
Idaho	4	1	5	38	1	39	44
Illinois	9	14	23	106	14	120	143
Indiana	10	10	20	114	6	120	140
Iowa	6	5	11	54	4	58	69
Kansas	12	7	19	66	1	67	86
Kentucky	12	2	14	91	9	100	114
Louisiana	14	6	20	56	13	69	89
Maine	4	0	4	9	4	13	17
Maryland	7	3	10	39	11	50	60
Massachusetts	4	1	5	21	5	26	31
Michigan	7	9	16	76	10	86	102
Minnesota	4	6	10	46	2	48	58
Mississippi	8	3	11	72	7	79	90
Missouri	17	9	26	92	17	109	135
Montana	8	2	10	19	5	24	34
Nebraska	3	3	6	54	4	58	64
Nevada	6	3	9	21	6	27	36
New Hampshire	0	0	0	6	1	7	7
New Jersey	8	3	11	49	18	67	78
New Mexico	5	21	26	42	9	51	77
New York	12	5	17	51	50	101	118
North Carolina	17	11	28	118	14	132	160
North Dakota	2	3	5	16	0	16	21
Ohio	18	12	30	133	9	142	172
Oklahoma	12	9	21	68	12	80	101
Oregon	12	6	18	38	11	49	67
Pennsylvania	18	9	27	98	10	108	135
Rhode Island	0	0	0	3	1	4	4
South Carolina	12	11	23	84	15	99	122
South Dakota	3	1	4	10	2	12	16
Tennessee	12	15	27	112	13	125	152
Texas	69	77	146	433	73	506	652
Utah	4	1	5	33	5	38	43
Vermont	2	0	2	8	0	8	10
Virginia	19	5	24	73	12	85	109
Washington	4	2	6	55	17	72	78
West Virginia	8	4	12	26	5	31	43
Wisconsin	6	7	13	50	7	57	70
Wyoming	6	7	13	22	4	26	39
U.S. Total	**495**	**397**	**892**	**3,544**	**569**	**4,113**	**5,005**
Puerto Rico	1	1	2	9	4	13	15

Source: FARS 2019 ARF

Fatality Analysis Reporting System

FARS contains data on every fatal motor vehicle traffic crash within the 50 States, the District of Columbia, and Puerto Rico. To be included in FARS, a traffic crash must involve a motor vehicle traveling on a public trafficway that results in the death of a vehicle occupant or a nonoccupant within 30 days of the crash. The Annual Report File (ARF) is the FARS data file associated with the most recent available year, which is subject to change when it is finalized the following year to the final version known as the Final File. The additional time between the ARF and the Final File provides the opportunity for submission of important variable data requiring outside sources, which may lead to changes in the final counts. More information on FARS can be found at www.nhtsa.gov/crash-data-systems/fatality-analysis-reporting-system.

The updated final counts for the previous data year will be reflected with the release of the recent year's ARF. For example, along with the release of the 2019 ARF, the 2018 Final File was released to replace the 2018 ARF. The final fatality count in motor vehicle traffic crashes for 2018 was 36,835, which was updated from 36,560 in the 2018 ARF. The number of large-truck crash fatalities from the 2018 Final File was 5,006, which was updated from 4,951 from the 2018 ARF.

The 2016 and 2017 Final Files have been amended, but this amendment did not change the overall number of fatal crashes or fatalities. However, the number of large-truck fatalities from the 2017 amended Final File was 4,906, which was updated from 4,905 from the 2017 Final File.

Crash Report Sampling System

NHTSA's National Center for Statistics and Analysis (NCSA) redesigned the nationally representative sample of police-reported traffic crashes, which estimates the number of police-reported injury and property-damage-only crashes in the United States. The new system, called CRSS, replaced the National Automotive Sampling System (NASS) General Estimates System (GES) in 2016. More information on CRSS can be found at www.nhtsa.gov/crash-data-systems/crash-report-sampling-system-crss.

Methodology Change for Estimating People Injured

NCSA changed the methodology of estimating people nonfatally injured in motor vehicle traffic crashes. The new approach combines people nonfatally injured from both FARS and NASS GES/CRSS. This is done by extracting people nonfatally injured in fatal crashes from FARS with people nonfatally injured in police-reported injury crashes from NASS GES/CRSS. The old approach extracted people nonfatally injured from only NASS GES/CRSS, regardless of crash severity. This change in methodology caused some estimates of people injured to change for prior years.

The suggested APA format citation for this document is:

National Center for Statistics and Analysis. (2021, May). *Large trucks: 2019 data.* (Traffic Safety Facts. Report No. DOT HS 813 110). National Highway Traffic Safety Administration.

For more information:

Motor vehicle traffic crash data are available from the National Center for Statistics and Analysis (NCSA), NSA-230. NCSA can be contacted at NCSARequests@dot.gov or 800-934-8517. NCSA programs can be found at www.nhtsa.gov/data. Additional data tools, such as the State Traffic Safety Information (STSI), Fatality and Injury Reporting System Tool (FIRST), and more can be found at https://cdan.nhtsa.gov/. To report a motor vehicle safety-related problem or to inquire about safety information, contact the Vehicle Safety Hotline at 888-327-4236 or www-odi.nhtsa.dot.gov/VehicleComplaint/.

Other fact sheets available from NCSA are *Alcohol-Impaired Driving, Bicyclists and Other Cyclists, Children, Motorcycles, Occupant Protection in Passenger Vehicles, Older Population, Passenger Vehicles, Pedestrians, Rural/Urban Comparison of Traffic Fatalities, School-Transportation-Related Crashes, Speeding, State Alcohol-Impaired-Driving Estimates, State Traffic Data, Summary of Motor Vehicle Crashes,* and *Young Drivers.* Detailed data on motor vehicle traffic crashes are published annually in *Traffic Safety Facts: A Compilation of Motor Vehicle Crash Data.* The fact sheets and Traffic Safety Facts annual report can be found at https://crashstats.nhtsa.dot.gov/.

U.S. Department of Transportation

National Highway Traffic Safety Administration

APPENDIX II

2020 Oklahoma Public Safety Crash Facts Book

Section 6. Miscellaneous Transportation

2020 Highway Safety Crash Facts Book

Miscellaneous Transportation

LARGE TRUCK CRASHES

Large Truck Crashes by County & Crash Injury Severity											
	Crash Injury Severity										
	Fatal		Serious		Minor		Possible		None		Total Crashes
County	OHP	Police	OHP	Police	OHP	Police	OHP	Police	OHP	Police	
Adair					3		3		4	2	12
Alfalfa	1				2				5		8
Atoka	1			2	5	1	5	3	14	33	64
Beaver	1				1		5		9		16
Beckham			1		2		13		38	6	60
Blaine			3		3		2		10	2	20
Bryan			1	1	5	6	3	8	13	46	83
Caddo	3		3		1		4		24	4	39
Canadian	2	1	4	1	11	1	10	10	72	62	174
Carter		1	2	1	5	2	9	2	23	21	66
Cherokee					2				5	3	10
Choctaw			2		3		4	2	3	4	18
Cimarron	1		1				4		10		16
Cleveland				1	1	8	8	11	44	71	144
Coal					2				5		7
Comanche				1	6	3	4	9	13	44	80
Cotton									8		8
Craig					2	1	4	1	19	11	38
Creek			2		8	2	11	1	50	15	89
Custer			5		4	1	4		47	5	66
Delaware			2		5	1	3	1	23	5	40
Dewey	1				3				6	1	11
Ellis					1				4		5
Garfield	2			1	4	2	1	3	8	59	80
Garvin	2		2		7		3		47	20	81
Grady	1	3	4	1	7	1	9	5	20	20	71
Grant	1		2		2		2		7	1	15
Greer									1		1
Harmon	1								3		4
Harper			2		1				5		8
Haskell					2		3		3	1	9
Hughes	1				1		1		9		12
Jackson								1	9	12	22
Jefferson	1								1		2
Johnston			1		2				7	6	16
Kay	1		1	1	2	1	8	1	17	19	51
Kingfisher	2		1		1		2	1	10	8	25
Kiowa			1		3				8		12
Latimer					1				5	2	8
LeFlore			3	1	3		6	3	15	26	57
Lincoln			3	2	4	1	9	2	33	7	61
Logan					1		2		32	8	43
Love	2				1		7		34	1	45
McClain	4		4		3	2	13	11	63	21	121

LARGE TRUCK CRASHES

Large Truck Crashes
by County & Crash Injury Severity

County	Crash Injury Severity										Total Crashes
	Fatal		Serious		Minor		Possible		None		
	OHP	Police	OHP	Police	OHP	Police	OHP	Police	OHP	Police	
McCurtain	1	1	2		4		10	2	28	4	52
McIntosh	1				5		6	1	22	5	40
Major	1		1		3				11		16
Marshall	1				2		1	1	9	2	16
Mayes	2		2		17	2	5	1	22	23	74
Murray			3	1			6	1	15	8	34
Muskogee	1		2	2	2	1	2	11	27	59	107
Noble	1		2		2	1	3	1	28	2	40
Nowata								1	9	3	13
Okfuskee	1			1	1		6		12	1	22
Oklahoma	3	3	16	12	37	27	64	60	444	468	1134
Okmulgee					2		2		11	13	28
Osage			1		3		2	1	7	4	18
Ottawa	1		4		5		8	2	34	6	60
Pawnee					2	1	2		7	2	14
Payne			2		3	2	3	3	17	17	47
Pittsburg			2	2	1	4	3	3	41	27	83
Pontotoc	1		1		2		4		5	4	17
Pottawatomie	1		3		7	2	6		36	14	69
Pushmataha			2	1					12	1	16
Roger Mills							2		4		6
Rogers	1	2	3		7		10	3	52	23	101
Seminole	4		1		5		8	1	11	18	48
Sequoyah	2		1		4	1	5	2	66	10	91
Stephens					2	1		4	6	12	25
Texas	2		1		1	1	6	2	17	21	51
Tillman			1				1		3		5
Tulsa	4	3	4	12	18	44	24	72	78	317	576
Wagoner	1			1	10	5	3	7	28	19	74
Washington			1	1				6	10	14	32
Washita	1		1		2		5		14		23
Woods							1		4	1	6
Woodward		1			1		1	2	7	16	28
	58	15	106	46	268	125	361	262	1883	1660	4784
Total	73		152		393		623		3543		4784

OHP indicates crashes worked by the Oklahoma Highway Patrol. These crashes are generally on rural roads and highways. Police indicates crashes worked by agencies (police, sheriff, campus police, etc.) other than the Oklahoma Highway Patrol. These crashes are generally worked within municipalities.

LARGE TRUCK CRASHES

Large Truck Crashes Highway Class & Injury Severity						
	Injury Severity					
Highway Class	Fatal	Serious	Minor	Possible	None	Total Crashes
Rural US Highway	15	23	56	63	247	404
Interstate Highway	23	35	85	185	1061	1389
Interstate Turnpike	1	11	25	28	135	200
Rural State Highway	13	21	47	54	209	344
County Road	3	6	30	31	178	248
City Street	5	21	72	118	932	1148
Urban US Highway	5	19	43	88	473	628
Urban State Highway	6	12	17	43	226	304
Non-Interstate Turnpike	2	4	18	13	80	117
Unknown					2	2
Total	73	152	393	623	3543	4784

Percent of Large Truck Crashes by Highway Class

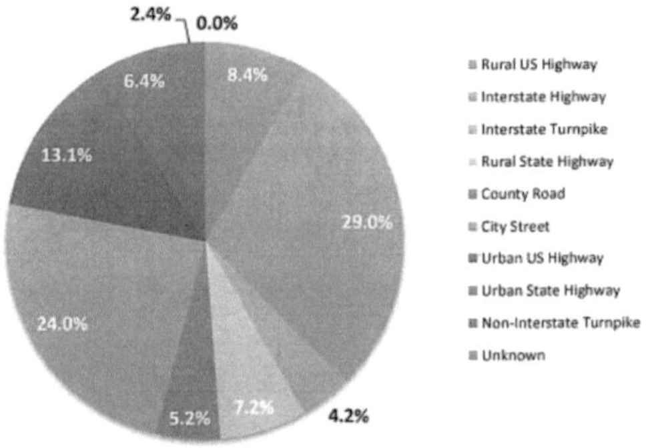

Large Truck Crashes Crash Injury Severity & Number of Vehicles Involved						
	Injury Severity					
Number of Vehicles	Fatal	Serious	Minor	Possible	None	Total Crashes
One Vehicle	10	32	121	116	827	1106
Two Vehicles	48	96	229	436	2561	3370
Three Vehicles	12	18	37	56	133	256
Four or More Vehicles	3	6	6	15	20	50
Total	73	152	393	623	3543	4784

DRIVERS IN LARGE TRUCK CRASHES

Drivers of Large Trucks in Crashes Driver Age & Driver Condition												
	Driver Condition											
Driver Age	Apparently Normal	Alcohol	Illegal Drugs	Medication	Very Tired	Sleepy	Sick	Dizzy/Faint	Emotional	Other	Unknown	Total Drivers
Unknown	10										329	339
16	5											5
17	4											4
18	9											9
19	14	1				1						16
20 - 24	258	1			1	4					9	273
25 - 29	446	1			2	6	1		2	1	10	469
30 - 34	476	4		1	2	4					18	505
35 - 39	483	1				5				3	15	507
40 - 44	514	5		1		6			1		13	540
45 - 49	546	7				5					10	568
50 - 54	529		1		1	7					18	556
55 - 59	527	1				2		1	2	3	14	550
60 - 64	390	1	1			4			1		9	406
65 - 69	203	1			1	4				1	3	213
70 - 74	72				1	1					2	76
75 - 79	40										1	41
80 - 84	8											8
85+	3											3
Total	4537	23	2	2	8	49	1	1	6	8	451	5088

Driver/Pedestrian Condition has 13 choices on the *Official Oklahoma Traffic Collision Report*. '02' Drinking-Ability Impaired and '03' Odor of Alcoholic Beverage are combined as Alcohol for this table. Also, if an Officer Affidavit is issued to the driver or a Medical Examiner Report indicates alcohol use, the Driver Condition is Alcohol.

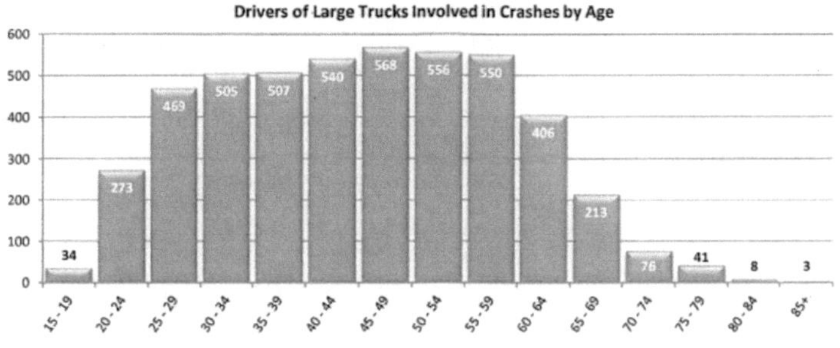

Does not include 339 drivers of unknown age.

DRIVERS IN LARGE TRUCK CRASHES

Contributing Factors of Drivers in Large Truck Crashes

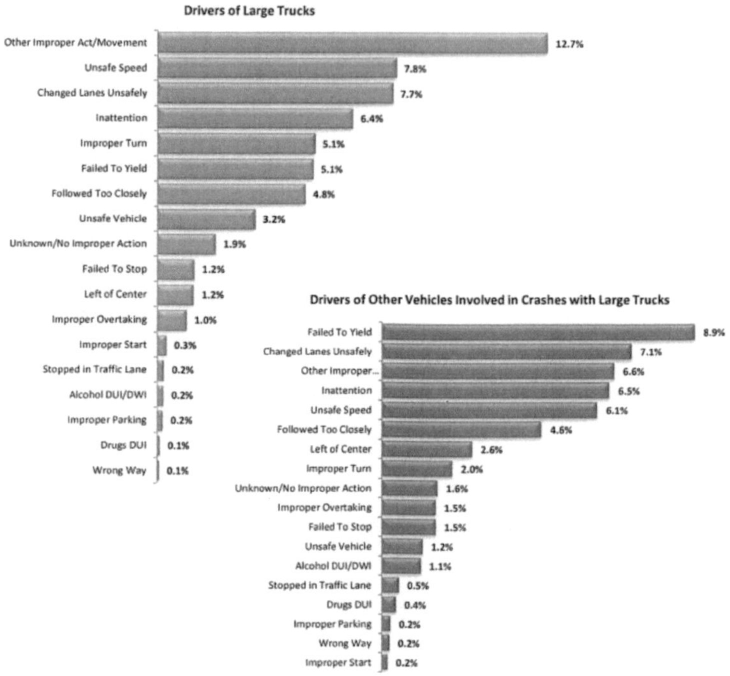

* The above results do not include the factor labeled "No Improper Action by Driver." On the current Oklahoma crash report form, every driver in a crash is assigned a contributing factor for the crash. If a driver is not at fault, "No Improper Action by Driver" is selected. In all crashes, this factor was assigned to 40.9% of large truck drivers and 47.0% of drivers of other vehicles involved in large truck crashes. "Other Improper Act/Movement" includes failure to signal, disregarding warning signal, improper lane use, improper backing, sleepy driver, failure to secure load, and unknown/other movements.

INDEX

R

S

T

U

NOTES

Made in the USA
Monee, IL
05 November 2026

67387500R00076